new river

bonnets, apple butter and moonshine

The Raising of a Fat Little Boy

D0815861

Charles Lytton

I would like to dedicate this book
to the two most important women in my life:
my lovely wife, Gail,
for hours of patience and proofreading,
and my mother
for her inspiration and for raising me.

CONTENTS

Foreword

I met Charles Lytton when I was a young teenager. I remember well how both he and his family immediately became my friends. They are all wonderful, loving people, and I regard Mrs. Lytton, Charles' mother, as my number two mother.

I spent many days and nights in their home and couldn't have been made to feel more welcome. They also had a cabin on the bank of New River where I spent some of the most memorable times of my life.

Charles is a big, strong man, and when we were all a bit younger we kindly referred to him as "Bull." For me, that nickname also had another connotation. He was always spinning yarns and telling tales, some of which were definitely intended to pull your leg. But then, you were never really sure.

Regardless, as long as I can remember, and it continues to this day, Charles has found a way to make me laugh, and I'm sure I'm not alone. He is a special human being, who has a fondness and gift for working with and developing our impressionable youth. He will always remain one of my lifelong friends, one I know I can count on through thick and thin. He knows he can count on me as well. I am so glad that he has chosen to capture many of his memories in print. I just hope that he had the good sense to leave out some of those that I remember, for heaven's sake.

Jim Bland

Franklin, NC

Introduction

My first understanding and appreciation of cooking food and its presentation came early on from my grandmother. Her house was cold and drafty in the winter. You could throw a cat through the cracks around the closed windows, and often snow blew under the doors. There was a wood or coal stove in every room except the kitchen, where a very big wood stove served as both a cook stove and source of heat.

Four or five o'clock every morning Grandmother went to the kitchen and started a fire. Now, often it got downright cold in there. Lots of the time, the water dipper was frozen in the drinking water bucket. Once the fire was started in the cook stove, the zinc water bucket was set on the stove, and the ice was melted and poured into the coffee pot. The remainder of the hot water got a chip or two of lye soap added. Soon, Daddy or Uncle Shorty would use this warm water to wash the mud and other stuff from the milk cow's teats.

As the cook stove started to get hot, it made a ring of warmth in the room. Grandmother set to making up fresh biscuits for breakfast. They were quickly put into the now hot oven. The very minute they came out of the oven, Grandmother slid the hog's slop bucket over to the oven. Then she pulled open the oven door and let it rest on the top of the slop bucket. She placed a dish towel on the oven door, and I set down. "Fat little boys get cold easy," she'd say. "This here is how I kept your daddy and uncles from freezing to death on cold mornings."

Mamaw would hand me a saucer with a homemade hot biscuit, right out of the oven, a biscuit with yellow cow butter running out the sides. Then she poured us both real hot cups of coffee. Her coffee was so black that you could have used it for ink; my coffee was equal parts fresh cream, sugar, cold water and coffee -- all great.

Grandmother always used that Luzianne coffee with chicory in it. "Old people out in the country still like the taste of chicory, don't you?"

"Why, yes ma'am, I do."

About the time our coffee was drunk and our first hot buttered biscuit was eat, you could hear others start to stir. That was our cue to start breakfast. I kept my seat on the oven door, and Mamaw started a cast-iron skillet of country ham, or salt cured middling bacon. Or, she might open a jar of canned sausage --just whatever she was in the mood for.

She handed me little pieces of meat right out of the pan, "Well how is that?"

"Mamaw, that is good" was my answer.

Once the meat was cooked, I helped her set it in the warming oven. (The warming oven is a small storage box over the woodstove that receives heat drifting up from the firebox.) She drained off about an inch of hot grease into another cast-iron pan and started making a bowl of hot gravy. I got to stir the gravy. I stood on a kitchen chair and stirred away, while she was cracking 10 or 15 eggs into the meat skillet. The fried eggs never had the chance to stick. They cooked as hard as Chinese arithmetic the second they hit the boiling grease. She rolled them eggs onto plates as eaters came into the kitchen.

Fried eggs, fried meat, hot biscuits, gravy and coffee were on the way. This is how I started about every day of my young life. I gained a great appreciation for how people on River Ridge lived. We wasted nothing, ate everything and never once went hungry. Never heard any complaining either.

As you read through this collection of stories and recipes, just try to think back and join me on the warm oven door. It was a hell of a place to start growing up and watch cooking and learn to appreciate the style unique to River Ridge. This is how I got to be so big and right manly developed.

A Glossary of Sorts

My friends tell me that some of the ways of living and cooking that are downright common to me may not be well-known to other people, so I guess to keep things simple I should explain a bit.

Yellow Cow Butter

In the spring, summer and early fall when there was lots of green grass to eat, all manner of milk cows gave thick yellowish cream. This translates into yellow butter, the norm for all country foods. But in the winter when cows started to be fed dry hay, corn fodder, and very little grain, the cream they produced did not have much color.

"Yellow cow butter" is the good kind. You took pride in your yellow, clover-printed cow butter and this is what you sold to people up and down the road. "Winter Butter" as some called it was what you ate at home. So, my reference to yellow cow butter is music to the ears of every red-necked boy that has ever milked a cow on a cold morning. He knows the expression "yellow cow butter" is an indicator of warmer days, green grass and easy times. Also, "yellow cow butter" comes from Guernsey

1

cows. Guernseys are from the Isle of Guernsey off the English coast. They are common all over the world. Guernsey milk is higher in beta carotene than all other cow milk. Beta carotene gives the milk an orange or yellowish hue – hence "Golden Guernsey milk." Some like it; some do not. Also, the milk is about 5 percent butterfat, so there is ample fat for making "yellow cow butter" all year round. Me, I like it. (The milk is white; only the fat part has more color.)

Popcorn to Test the Hot Lard

People who don't cook with lard often may just not know how important it is to have the heat just right. We used a little trick. We put three or four popcorn kernels in the lard to indicate the proper cooking temperature. When the lard is hot enough to pop the popcorn, you can put chicken or green tomatoes into the lard and your food won't be too greasy.

Today there are all kinds of thermometers for measuring the temperature of cooking oil, but in my mama's day, you only had experience and popcorn.

A Trotline

A trotline is a method of fishing where you use many hooks, instead of setting on the riverbank and casting with a pole , and therefore using only one hook. A trotline is a strong cord tied to a root on the shore and stretched across the river. About every three feet along the cord you tie a fishhook. That way, you can put bait in for catfish throughout the whole channel.

Cracklin

Cracklin is a pork byproduct made from waste fat, which is ground much like sausage and then cooked. Once all the fat is rendered out, the remaining product is the cracklin, which when it is cooled is light brown in color and very crunchy.

The cracklin made from the fat near the skin is very hard and difficult to eat, but that made from leaf fat is puffier, with none of the animal's skin. This is the cracklin that in the old days was heavily salted and added to cornbread for flavor. Sometimes cracklin was eaten like potato chips are today.

Gigging

Gigging is an illegal form of fishing. It is done on a very dark night when there is little or no moon. The headlight from an old car is used to blind the fish while the boat is maneuvered into place. A gig, with four or five sharp points, is stuck into the fish's back. Each gig point is between six and eight inches long with a sharp barb on the end. Gigging is a way to collect a large number of fish in one outing.

NOT BY BREAD ALONE

Cat-Headed Biscuits

About every morning of my mother's life she crawled out of bed before anyone else and set to making fresh hot biscuits for breakfast. Mom had what she called a "202 soup can." This can had two important roles in the biscuit-making process. In the bottom she had poked about 100 pinholes. This was her flour sifter. The open end of the soup can was her biscuit cutter. (The can was her flour-measuring cup, too.)

On the table she measured out eight or nine cans of flour. Then she dumped her baking soda and baking powder into the soup can and sifted it over the flour. "It mixes better this way," Mom laughed. Well, after she had made the flour into dough and rolled it out about 3/8" thick, she picked up her soup can again to cut the biscuits.

The can cut 36 biscuits the exact same size and shape. Thirty-six is what fit onto the baking sheet. Yes, she made 36 hot biscuits each morning. If she had done everything exactly right, they would puff up to the size of a "cat's head." Thus, "Cat-headed Biscuits"! All the leftover dough was mashed out into a smallish flat loaf or "hoe-cake" and baked in a small cast-iron pan. Elmer always carried the hoecake to work for lunch. A hoecake sandwich is a prized thing.

Dear old Mom jumped out of the bed every morning for 25 years and made hot homemade biscuits for breakfast. Exactly 36 biscuits cut with a 202 size can fit on the baking sheet. We were good eaters. Appetite, what is that? I do not know: we just ate everything.

Here is what you need:

- Two cups of all-purpose flour
- One cup of whole wheat flour
- 1/2 teaspoon salt
- 4 1/2 teaspoons of double-acting baking power
- Two teaspoons of sugar
- 3/4 teaspoon of cream of tarter
- 1/4 - 1/2 cup of lard
- One cup of buttermilk
- One egg

Now, here is what you do:

- Turn on the oven to 450 degrees.
- Pour the flour, salt, baking powder, cream of tartar, and sugar into a flour sifter and slowly sift everything onto the dough board.
- Dig a small hole in the middle of the mixture and dump in your lard. With a knife and a fork cut the lard and flour together until the mixture looks kind of grainy or like pieces of broken rice.
- On a floured dough board, add the buttermilk and start kneading the mixture.
- Do not knead but about one minute, and then carefully pat the dough into a ball.
- Again on a floured surface, pat the ball out flat and take your roller and roll the dough down to about 3/8 inch.
- Cut out the biscuits with a 202 soup can and place them in a large cast-iron skillet. A biscuit baking pan will do, if you don't have a cast-iron one.
- Cook for about 15 minutes or until the tops are brown.

Serving suggestions:

Why, there is no recommendation! You can eat them right out of the oven. You can eat them with gravy. You can eat them with anything hot or cold. A fresh biscuit is one of the most perfect and complete foods anywhere.

Daddy's Hot Rolls

When Elmer – that's my dad -- took a notion to make hot rolls everyone was happy. I, too, was happy, for two reasons. Daddy was a great hot roll maker. He would clean up everything, and you knew to stay out of his way. He was prone to throw things if you got to bothering him. His first requirement was to be about half to two-thirds drunk. Being drunk was just the way he liked to be. You could tell when he was about ready to start cooking. His rather large nose got so red that you could see the blood veins in it. His cheeks took on a kind of blue look, too. Yes, he was about ready.

Before Elmer could start any project he had to scream at everyone and give most of us a good sound cussing. "It is your fault that there is no yeast," or "By damn when did you hide my roll pans." One of my favorites was: "By damn you made the bread fall."

It was not as bad as it sounds; everyone just got to the point that they paid no attention to him. One day, as an adult, I asked him how he made the rolls. He hemmed and hawed around some and never gave me much of anything to go on. To

10

Daddy's credit, he had no recipe. He just made rolls by ear, kind of like a piano player plays the piano by ear. Lots of country cooking was done "by ear."

When I lived at the cabin on the river I tried to make rolls a few times. Never once did they turn out like his. My rolls were kind of like yeasty crackers. One of the things I did differently was I tried to make them when I was sober. That may have been one of the problems. Me, I find yeast rolls to be great, if someone else is willing to make them. I just can't do it.

None of my siblings or Mom has much to say about how they were made, but the one thing we are in agreement on is their goodness. One of my siblings said: "You put two hot light rolls in a dish, pull them in half and add some butter. Once the butter has started to melt, take the tops off of the rolls, and expose the butter. Carefully spoon corned beef hash into the bowl until the gravy is just even with the tops of the rolls. You want those tops to resemble two sunny-side-up fried eggs."

With this description I cannot think of anything else to say other than, "Um, um good!"

One of my many favorite ways to eat Daddy's rolls was to put two in the bottom of a bowl and cover both with hot pinto beans. Then, I add two or three tablespoons of chowchow and cover the top with chopped onions. I also like to put on a layer of black pepper. Now, the rolls and beans are ready when you are.

One last thing about Daddy's rolls was volume. He did not make just one real big pan full. Elmer cooked a pan of rolls for every house on the hill. After all of the cussing and hollering, everyone was ready for hot rolls, too.

This is where I usually start with "Here is what you need." This time, though, you'll just have to look up the recipe in a cookbook. Neither Momma nor I can remember much more than flour, fresh yeast and warm water. If they don't turn out the first time, just look around and holler at the closest person. That may help.

I can bet Elmer's recipe was much like your mom's recipe – or as some used to say, "receipt." Everyone I talked to said the secret to good hot rolls is making a big pan full and lots of practice.

Long Shop Cornbread

Mom and Grandmother had a way of using everything. I cannot recall a time when there was more than a scrap of eatable food in the hog slop bucket.

"You ort to be eating the food up. I don't care if you don't like it," Grandmother would say. So you ate the stuff. I can remember being about 11 or 12 years old and going to friends' houses. We would set down to eat, and I ate everything that I was given, even the slick okra. Hell, I thought that I had to eat it. It was so slick that the hogs wouldn't eat, so I had to.

This recipe is an example of what I mean about using up leftovers. Today, though, when I make this dish I use store-bought ingredients. Also, these days I only use drained spinach and add store-bought shredded cheese on the top just before I serve it.

Well I think it is happening to me! I think that am turning into a town person. "Why?" you are asking. Well sometimes when I make cornbread I use some frozen broccoli rather than cold greens. I also use cottage cheese rather than buttermilk. It is simple and it is good, too.

Here is what you need:

- All the old cold salt-cured bacon left over from breakfast, crumbled up
- One cup of last night's leftover greens
- Old ham from last night's supper chopped into small pieces
- Four fresh eggs
- A big onion, top and all, chopped right small
- Buttermilk
- Two cups of self-rising cornmeal
- Butter, lard and some salt

Now, here is what you do:

- Build up a good fire in the wood cook stove and pre-heat the oven to somewhere around 350 to 400 degrees.
- Put about 1/2 cup of lard in a cast-iron pan and put it in the oven to get it hot.
- Make sure the greens are well drained.
- When the grease is hot, into a bowl put the eggs, bacon, ham, onion and cornmeal.
- Pour in some buttermilk.
- Adjust the buttermilk with the moisture of the greens. You may need none, and you may need 1/2 to 1/4 cup.
- If the bacon and ham are strong with salt, do not add more salt.
- Stir up the mixture very slowly, scraping the sides of the bowl. Do not stir more than 15 or 20 times.
- Spoon the mixture into the center of the cast-iron pan.
- Bake for about 30 or 40 minutes or until it is done.

THE GARDEN

OF

EATING

That Quintessential Berry: The Food of the Gods!

There is no finer food than the tomato biscuit. As a child growing up I was exposed to some of the best food there ever was. Tenderloin, chicken-fried steak, and mashed potatoes turned yellow with homemade cow butter -- all pale compared to the first fresh tomato biscuit of the season. I will admit that by fall I had eaten about all of them I wanted. I guess that happens after about three or four thousand; your taste just seems to wear out.

Now, I do not know who invented the tomato biscuit, but I bet there is a place in heaven for this person. I also don't know which style of cooking the tomato biscuit falls under, but I think that it must be a French invention. To my way of thinking the French put a lot of care into their food. A good and proper tomato biscuit takes a lot of care and preparation.

Another thing, I do not want to be down on town people. I need to be real careful here. You see, I am now one of them. You know the other kind of people, "Town People." I try not to be, but here I am. Well anyway, true town people have no clue what I am talking about here. Just you wait and see. Some readers will ask you, "What is he talking about?" Don't be surprised if it takes a while to get an answer. I am just remembering my first long-awaited tomato biscuit.

For the sake of everything that is good and tasty, do not rush the process. And if you lose your resolve and eat your first tomato on light bread, do not tell people. They may take to calling you a townie. There will be lots of time for tomato sandwiches later on. You know, the ones where the sliced bread is hot and toasted with fresh fried bacon and red-eared leaf lettuce with lots of mayonnaise. Well, enough is enough. I need to go to the garden and check out the pantry.

Before we look at the recipe, though, there is one sad story wrapped up here I do not want you to repeat. Once I had found the most perfect red tomato and hurried into the house for my first tomato biscuit. When I picked out the best biscuit on the plate I realized that I have been deceived by store-bought canned biscuits. You could tell by the smell, texture and general appearance. I was forced to eat a store- bought biscuit, not a true cat-headed fresh homemade one. You talk about a letdown. So keep an eye on your mom.

Here is what you need to do:

- Find one dead-ripe, red tomato about the size of a softball. Look the garden over for it. For me, it needs to be a red one; nothing says tomato like a big red one. It needs to be free of all blemishes and have a small stem. I know that this is a lot of work, but the payoff is worth it. Don't just go and pick it. You must wait and watch it until it is as red as a strawberry. As the day for the first tomato biscuit draws close, look the house over and make sure there is plenty of flour, both sweet milk and buttermilk and fresh butter. If you have to go to town, then go on today and get the right stuff. When the selected tomato is at its perceived zenith of ripeness, very carefully pick it and carry it home. Do not wash it. Just carefully wipe it off with a dishtowel and set it aside out of the sun.

- Using the tried and true family recipe for biscuits, bake up one pan full. Better yet, get your mother to do this step, since she has the most experience. This is not the place or time for an amateur. Make sure your mom makes buttermilk biscuits. They are the softest for sure. We do not want any screw-ups at this stage.

- Here is an important item, often overlooked. When the biscuits are done, you want the two from the center of the pan. They are the tenderest and have enjoyed the rise to perfection with the help of the other biscuits in the pan.

- Lay the two best biscuits on a plate and cut them in half and put one large hunk of butter on each biscuit. Replace the top half of the biscuit and wait for the butter to melt and soak into the bread. You can turn over the biscuits a few times to make sure the butter is soaking into the top.

- Now and only now, approach the tomato with the knife. Carefully slice the whole tomato into slices about ½ inch think. Select the two center slices and put one on each biscuit. Cover each tomato slice with black pepper and add some salt.

Serving suggestions:

Slowly eat the tomato biscuit and wash it down with sweet milk. Nothing else is needed for this meal. NO, nothing! Except some peace and quiet where you can concentrate on your tomato biscuit.

The Making of Sauerkraut and Brine Pickles

One of our fall rituals was making homemade sauerkraut and brine pickles. I read not long ago that from 1900 until 1940 the average American ate more than 50 pounds of cabbage per year. Today, we Americans only eat about 10 pounds of cabbage per year.

In the 60s and 70s our whole family on River Ridge was doing our best to keep up the local, state and national average. Our consumption was measured in how many gallons we dipped out of the barrels. Mom and Daddy dipped it out at least once and sometimes two times per week. Daddy said that it was good for your innards. I can tell you how much we made -- exactly one 55-gallon barrel and two 20-gallon earthen crocks full each fall, always stored in the root cellar.

Sauerkraut started in the early spring. My Uncle Shorty usually planted more than eight rows of cabbage across the garden behind the chicken house. Somehow it seemed like everybody just showed up at Shorty's to start making sauerkraut. The first step was to get everything cleaned up for the new cabbage. This was by far the hardest part. I was youngest, so clean up was my job. I had to take a small bucket and dip all of last year's sauerkraut out of the crocks and barrel. In a good year it smelled as bad as cleaning the hog pen. There was always some leftover sauerkraut in the bottom of the barrel. Also, there was about a half a barrel of thick, ropey, old salty cabbage juice. Together the cabbage and juice had taken to getting right slick. The amazing thing here was that we were still eating the sauerkraut the day before; it was still good. I dipped out all of the saltwater and leftover kraut and hauled it to the woods. I had to rake old leaves over the sauerkraut to keep the smell from coming back into the house.

Next, grownups wrestled the barrel out of the cellar and started cleaning it with fresh water and baking soda until it looked okay. By afternoon it was left to set in the sun while all the busted heads of cabbage were brought to the willow tree. (Solid heads were left in the garden; they would be buried later. To preserve the better heads for winter, we dug a shallow pit lined with hay and straw. We put good cabbage heads on straw, roots up and then covered with straw. Later, one simply pulled them up one at a time by the roots to eat them.) Once the cabbage was sorted and enough had been amassed to begin, the barrel was put back in the cellar.

We chopped the fresh heads of cabbage and rubbed them with salt until they started to ooze water. Everyone had a big, razor-sharp knife. (Richer people had store-bought cabbage cutters.) All day long you looked out for your fingers and hands. Then we dumped five-gallon buckets of salt and cabbage into the newly cleaned barrel. This was repeated until the barrel was full almost to the top.

Once the barrel was full, we put a board on top and weighted it down with rocks. The cabbage was pressed to the bottom and a layer of salt brine came to the top. We added another layer of salty cabbage. There could be no air in the barrel. We put an unbroken raw egg in the water, and if it sank we added more salt until it floated.

This was a nasty job. About the only thing that came around were flies. I tell you all this to make you realize that making salt brine cucumber pickles was even worse. We went to all the gardens and picked every cucumber left. Some were big, some were small, but every cucumber was brought to the willow tree in the backyard and washed and cut into four pieces. The only criterion for these cucumbers was they could not be yellow. The hogs got the yellow ones.

Once quartered, the cucumbers went into either a big earthen crock or a small wooden barrel. A handful of rock salt was added, and very quickly lots of cucumber juice happened. We put in more cucumbers and more salt was added and stirred until the crock was full. Sometimes we dropped hard green apples in the salt brine with cucumbers. In about three weeks you had sauerkraut and brine pickles.

We also made a kind of garlic dill pickles in one of the smaller earthen crocks. You see, we did not need more than about 20 gallons of salt brine garlic dill pickles. We added whole dill flowers to the salt mix, and then pulled fresh garlic from the ground near the gate leading to the barn. No more than a quart of fresh garlic pieces were needed. Now, I ain't pulling your leg here. Only the hardiest of the seasoned drunk men could eat the salty garlic dill pickles.

We made sauerkraut and pickles until I was way up in high school. I am a great believer in old family traditions, but every once in a while a tradition comes along that just needs to be laid aside and forgotten. This was one.

To eat the sauerkraut, you just took off the rocks and boards, and reached down through the slimy water until you found enough sauerkraut for supper. Then you put the boards and rocks back on the top and stood there until the water covered the rocks. You see, the boards and rocks had to rest on the top of the cabbage.

Only the Lord above could help you if you got in a hurry and let one of the rocks slip off the boards and fall to the bottom of the barrel. I reckon you would just be kilt on the spot or worse. You might be made to swim down there and find that rock. I was never in too much of a hurry at the rock-putting-back time.

Once you had finished in the cellar and you had your kraut, you put it in the sink and washed off as much salt as you could, then soaked it in fresh clean water, the longer the better. If you skipped this step you were going to drink water and lots of it for a week. Once it was free of most of the salt, you just cooked it.

As for the pickles, I've seen men come from all over for them. It was said that they would cure a hangover. How they would cure anything is beyond me. If you got one or two pickles down, you'd drink a gallon of water for sure.

Now, I liked the salty apples, but we did not make many of them. I think my uncles were more into the aspect of hangover treatment. At times we had a lot of them, both salt pickles and hangovers.

Uncle Shorty ate kraut and weenies two or three times a week for most of his life. He said that it kept the worms cut up in him.

Here is what you need:

- One very large cast-iron skillet
- A big spoon of lard
- Send one very strong-stomached person, (preferably a World War II veteran) to the kraut barrel in the cellar to extract about one or two gallons of sauerkraut. The kraut is mostly water so it is going to shrink up a lot. Salt cured ham or bacon
- One package of hotdogs

Now, here is what you do:

- Soak and rinse the kraut with fresh water at least three times for at least 30 minutes each time, and then put it in a colander to drain.
- Fry up about one pound of home-cured bacon or ham. You can set this aside or eat it any way you want. You see, the main thing needed is the drippings for the recipe. If you don't have the bacon or ham you can use a large scoop of lard. If you don't have lard, Crisco may be substituted, but it won't be as good. I hope you do not have to go this route.
- Cut a full package of hotdogs and cut into 1/2- inch pieces and set aside.
- You may chop up one or two very large onions and put in the drippings. This is up to you. It is not required, but heartily encouraged. In the spring use the onion, tops and all. They add some color.
- Once the drippings are very hot, and the onions are in, let the onion cook for few minutes.
- Carefully add in all the cabbage at one time. (If the drippings take to smoking, you are a little too hot.)
- When a few of the cabbages are starting to get a little brown look about them, add in all of the hotdogs.
- Cook until the hot dogs are all kind of rolled up and the cabbage is cooked down to about three quarters of its original size.

Serving suggestions:

Serve your fried sauerkraut with a big piece of cracklin cornbread, pinto beans with onions chopped up on top, strong yellow cow butter, and a large glass of cold buttermilk. It might even be nice to have a ham slice or a few leftover bacon slices. Fried potatoes are good with sauerkraut, too. Afterwards, it would be good to have a fried apple pie cooked until it is brown around the edges with a cup of black coffee.

Cabbage — Fried or Boilt

We ate an awful lot of fried cabbage. We planted 200 or 300 cabbage plants each year. Yes, we planted a lot. The only person who planted more was Uncle Shorty. Now, he planted cabbage. He had eight rows across the garden. Later, in school we learned that between Daddy and Shorty we grew enough cabbage to reach to the moon and most of the way back. Sadly, we ate all of it. Not really sad for us, but sad for everyone around us. Some days I was right strong, if you catch my drift.

Also, it is very important that everyone in the house is eating the same meal. If possible, everyone in the neighborhood should be enjoying boiled cabbage and pinto beans at about the same time. I can assure you conversation is going to become a gaseous affair.

I've included both recipes. The one for fried cabbage is next door, and you turn the page for the one for boilt. You can choose!

Here is what you need for fried cabbage:

- Walk the garden and pick two cabbage heads that have busted open. Save the solid ones for burying.

- Salt and black pepper

- A big cast-iron skillet (I have so much iron in my blood that I sometimes fear I might rust.)

- While in the garden, pull three or four onions.

- You can use one cup of lard, ham or bacon drippings.

Now, here is what you do:

- Shred up the cabbage with a vegetable grater. Save the cabbage stalks for the kids to eat with salt.

- Chop up the onions.

- Once the lard or drippings are hot, add in the onions and toss them around a few times.

- Add in all of the cabbage and slowly stir.

- Let the cabbage cook on medium heat until it has cooked down to about 1/3 its original volume. If you can look into the skillet and tell that it was once cabbage, it isn't cooked enough.

Here is what you need for boilt cabbage (no, not boiled, boilt):

- Go to the garden and pick two busted heads of cabbage
- A two-gallon stew pot
- Salt and pepper
- Streaked fatback meat

Now, here is what you do:

- Put about 1/2 gallon of water in the stew pot.
- Add in one tablespoon of salt.
- Add one teaspoon of black pepper.
- Cut slices about halfway through about a 1/2 pound piece of fat-streaked meat and put it in the pan.
- Turn the stove on to boil.
- Once the fat meat is boiling good, (DO NOT TAKE IT OUT OF THE PAN, just keep on cooking it.) start adding in the fresh cabbage.
- Boil the cabbage until it is no longer green. Cut the heat down when the cabbage gets a little red tinge to it.
- Now, cut the heat down to low and let them "Cabbages Boil Down."
- They are not done as long as you can figure out what they were.

Serving suggestions:

My daddy liked the cabbage to be a little slick with lots of black pepper and vinegar. Anytime you have cabbage, you need a dish of brown beans with homemade chowchow. Sweet tea and cornbread and fresh cow butter are a must, the kind of butter Grandmother has just made with the little clover print on top.

Here is something good for your heart. When the cabbage or brown beans were served, about everyone around the table just went for a hunk of the fat streaked meat. I just loved the boiled fat meat. Truly the supper of a champion!

Fried Cabbage Long Shop Style, not Uncle Shorty Style

Some old foods are just too good to forget about. Take cabbage for example. Growing up, cabbage was a part of everyday. If you were not planting cabbage you were pulling weeds out of the cabbage.

You know, Uncle Shorty liked cabbage like no one I have ever known. He would drive over to the Community of Bent Mountain every fall and buy a pickup truck load of cabbage. There were a thousand heads in the garden, and they were good cabbages too. But Bent Mountain Cabbage is the best cabbage in the world. Shorty would say, "It is sweeter than most and more crunchy and packed full of juice."

Well, all of Uncle Shorty's appreciation of cabbage is not wasted on me. I, too, like my cabbage, but over the years I have begun to fix it a little different than the regular fried cabbage. The roots of the recipe are still in the garden behind the house and using the stuff that you have.

29

I like to cook this in the very early summer, outside on the gas grill. Our local wine tasting group likes this recipe for cabbage.

It takes about 35 minutes to cook. Please do not overcook the cabbage. When finished, the cabbage should have a slight crunchy texture.

Here is what you need:

- One large head of cabbage
- Three medium onions from the garden
- Six stalks of celery
- Three or four tablespoons of garlic (Today I get it out of a little jar in the refrigerator.)
- A small handful of each: fresh rosemary, basil, thyme, and parsley. Please note: fresh herbs do not have a strong flavor, like dried herbs.
- One cup olive oil
- One tablespoon of cayenne pepper
- Salt and pepper to taste
- A big handful of fresh chives, if you have them
- Six or eight green cherry tomatoes
- Eight to ten red ripe cherry tomatoes
- A sprig or two of fresh mint
- A cup of coarsely grated parmesan cheese
- The biggest cast-iron skillet you have; a cast-iron Dutch oven works well
- A cabbage shredder

Now, here is what you do:

- Put an ounce of the olive oil in the cast-iron skillet and let it start to get warm.

- Chop everything into uniform pieces and set aside. I just chop cabbage, onion and celery pepper on a vegetable shredder and set it all aside in a bowl. Pour the remainder of the olive oil over the chopped cabbage and let it set until ready for the skillet.

- The tomatoes I cut in half and set aside in separate bowls.

- For the rosemary, thyme and parsley, I take out the big stems and coarsely chop what's left and put into another bowl.

- Once the cast-iron skillet is hot and the olive oil is thinking about starting to smoke, dump in the cabbage, onion and celery. Add salt and pepper. It does look like a lot but it cooks down quickly.

- When the cabbage starts to take on a transparent look, add in the green tomatoes.

- In minute or two sprinkle the fresh herbs over the skillet and stir. I like for the herbs to still have some shape and form when the cabbage is cooked.

- You may want to pull out a little and taste for salt and pepper.

- Once the cabbage has lost most of the color and the onions are cooked, add the ripe tomatoes.

- Let this cook until the red tomatoes are soft and losing their form. It is finished.

- Dump the cabbage into a large serving bowl. Sprinkle the Parmesan cheese over the top and garnish with sprigs of mint and some chives.

Serving suggestions:

I serve this cabbage recipe with Sauvignon Blanc. I also like the Fumé style wine. The light oak flavor goes well with this dish.

The Old Cook Stove and Creamed Potatoes and Peas

There was an old wood cook stove setting near the very front of the bus we used as fishing headquarters down by the river. It was kept outside because it didn't fit through the door. The old trailer hitch on the bus served as a table to set important stuff on, like your beer, your cigarettes, Bull of the Woods, or anything else of lesser importance. Sometimes even food.

I saw my last wild hazelnuts on the bank just behind the old stove. If the stove had not been placed there, I might have missed those nuts. The bushes are all gone now. Actually, come to think of it, they were not wild. They were planted by Granddaddy Ervin at the head of the path leading to the railroad.

Sometimes Mom came down to the bus in the mornings. It took an hour to get the stove properly heated up where you could bake biscuits. She cooked bacon and sausage, baked bread and made homemade gravy. Yes, outside gravy is much better than inside gravy; I think the early morning light has a lot to do with that.

At the old bus, we kept fishing rods, boat paddles, trotlines, canned food, cooking pans, bedding and other stuff. Early in the life of the bus the whole family came. Daddy paddled the boat. I think the little outboard motor made his neck hurt or something. He did not like reaching back to hold the drive handle, so he paddled everywhere he went. Maybe it made him think of a slower, quieter time. I cast a plug out as he paddled.

We rarely spoke a word. Instead, we just watched the river. I always caught a few small ones. Daddy said: "Why in the world do you waste your time with them little ones when you could be cat fishing?"

Often we were headed for the Tommy Bottom to pick tomatoes, cantaloupes, ears of corn and beans and dig up fresh potatoes. In the spring, we picked peas, too. We cooked up whatever we had on the outside cook stove. Sometimes we fried fresh fish right off of the trotlines.

Once in a while, Mom would come to the river and dispatch some of us to the garden – mostly it was just me. I was to pick about a bushel of peas in the shell and dig up a peck of early red potatoes. When I came back to the bus, we shelled the peas and then washed both peas and new potatoes in the river. Mom made new potatoes and creamed peas with small onions right there on the riverbank.

You know, today I, too, paddle everywhere I go. I do think there is some truth in the saying, "When you grow up you do what your parents did." I paddle only on the left side of the canoe like Daddy; I am fat like Daddy. Why, I even wear one of those flat-looking hats like Daddy.

Here is what you need:

- About ten smallish new red potatoes or three regular ones cut into one-inch pieces. You don't have to peel them unless you just like them peeled.
- Six or seven small green onions. Cut off the tops and then cut the onions into 1/2 " pieces.
- Salt -- about a teaspoon is enough, but you can salt to taste.
- At least one quart of fresh peas
- Three cups of fresh whole milk, with the cream on it if you got it
- Fresh yellow cow butter -- at least two large hunks from a pound block.
- Two tablespoons of flour
- A little cold water
- Pepper to taste

Now, here is what you do:

- Put the potatoes in a pan with one tablespoon of salt and boil them for about 10 minutes or until they are tender.
- Start the peas and onions boiling in another pan with salt.
- When both the peas and onions and the potatoes are done, drain them and put them into a large saucepan.
- Add the two cups of milk and the hunks of butter and cook until the milk and butter come to a low boil. Then set the pan off high heat.
- Make up some flour paste with cold water and flour, and pour some of it over the peas and potatoes. Add just enough paste to thicken them up.
- Keep stirring, but real easy so as not to break the peas, until they start to thicken.
- Add more salt and black pepper to suit yourself.

Green Bean Casserole

I know that town people may not understand this story, but I like it; I hope you do, too. Just one piece of background information to set the stage: on River Ridge my diet was limited. Now, I ate my fill each and every day. But you ate about the same thing every day of your life. You ate what you had. Corn, beans, potatoes, tomatoes, peppers, and green beans were the main staples. You ate them raw in the spring, fresh cooked in the summer and canned in the winter. I can almost say with certainty that we ate no more than 12 different foods. Your choice of food did not change.

As Aunt Maude once said, "Yesterday we had brown beans and cornbread; today we are having cornbread and brown beans." People all over River Ridge just waited for the first mess of fresh green beans. It was a welcome change from last year's canned beans.

People bragged on who could raise the first mess of green beans and the first red ripe tomato. It was a sure sign of your gardening skills. When spring came to River Ridge everyone

35

went to work on the garden. Some people's minds take to thinking about the opposite sex, but on the Ridge we took to thinking about gardening and fresh green beans, creamed peas and new red potatoes and tomatoes. We pulled last winter's dead weeds in the garden, piled them up and set them afire.

Pretty soon old Washington Chadbourn came with a pair of big horses and plowed. Everybody grabbed their hoe and started. As soon as the ground got a little warm, we put two or three rows of green beans in. About every ten days or two weeks, we planted two or three more rows, both bush beans and pole beans.

We ate fresh green beans from early summer until frost about every way there is to eat them. It was kind of like "Bubba Gump and his shrimp." First, we ate them boiled with fat salt pork. They are good that way; cooked until they are done or until you cannot tell the contents of the pan from green mush. I loved them.

As the summer wore on, though, you kind of lost your liking for green beans. After about ten bushels they just don't taste the same. Some foods you got kind of tired of eating. But Uncle Lake said, "You eat anything that will make a turd." Please keep in mind: Uncle Lake was the better educated and more worldly of my uncles.

Then one summer day, Mom took a big cast-iron skillet out of the stove, and we had baked green beans -- pretty good. I now think my favorite way to eat green beans is the "Green

Bean Casserole," and that is right simple, too. Daddy said that this is the way they eat green beans in town. Damn them town people. They do have it made, don't they?

Well anyway, it was a Saturday morning in late summer and we were about ready to go to town for groceries. Mom came out of the house carrying a sheet of paper torn from a magazine. Daddy said, "What in the world is that? Oh expletive, you ain't going to make that are you? It just don't sound good."

No matter, she did make the first Green Bean Casserole I ever saw. I ate a gallon at the first meal. My! My! What a change from boiled green beans, pickled green beans, green beans mixed with brown beans – well, you get the picture.

Today everybody can just buy or make Green Bean Casserole, so much so that it is old hat or –- what is that French word? Passé. I almost never make it anymore. Times do change, don't they? I think that keeping your eye on the most insignificant things is a way to document movement in the time line.

Green beans -- I can bet that you never thought about them as a way to document change, now did you? But, I can still see that old carry-all with a kid's head stuck out each window going off to the grocery store on Saturday morning; Mom, setting up front with her "Green Bean Casserole" recipe in her hand and Old Elmer just shaking his head. The excitement of having the casserole was like what you'd feel today about the news of an ice cream cake after supper.

Here is what you need:

- About one small grocery bag full of fresh green beans
- 1/2 teaspoon of black pepper, or more if you like pepper
- Red pepper, if you like. Daddy didn't.
- A cup of whole cream
- Some soy sauce
- A can of cream of mushroom or cream of celery soup
- A few crumbled slices of crispy bacon
- Two or three tablespoons of bacon drippings
- Now here is the secret ingredient -- one can French-fried onions.

Now, here is what you do:

- In a large bowl mix everything but the French-fried onions.
- Put the bowl in the oven at 350 degrees and bake for about 1/2 hour.
- At about 25 minutes, take it out of the oven and pour on the onions; then put the pan back in the oven for a few minutes to let the onions brown.

Serving suggestions:

Serve with cornbread, coleslaw, fresh-dug onions, fried potatoes, sweet milk, and fresh sliced tomatoes. If they are available, a dish of fried apples would be nice. A hot, cat-headed biscuit and yellow cow butter. And a dish or two of fresh peach or blackberry cobbler with cream.

Daddy's Baked Potatoes

Mr. Vance Buckshot ran a small Grade "C" dairy not too far from my home on River Ridge. He had to have a good springhouse, because this was where he stored milk waiting to be shipped. It stayed very cool in there -- about 50 degrees or so, the temperature of the cool spring water coming straight out of the earth. The inside of the springhouse was no more than 10 feet by 10 feet and the depth of the water was about 12 to 14 inches.

More than once, on hot summer days, Mr. Buckshot said they caught Daddy lying down in the cold water in the milk house with his belly just above the water line. He would have a crock of milk turned up drinking the cream off the top. A man has got to eat and drink, doesn't he, if he is to grow properly with good teeth and all?

Daddy could eat more than just milk and cream. He always served his rolls with baked potatoes. The rolls were interesting in their own right. Daddy could have been a professional yeast roll maker. He made them about every Saturday. They were so good with gravy of any kind. They just seemed to match up well with white milk gravy. As you know from what I wrote earlier, for the rolls you are on your own, but I do know how he made baked potatoes. They were real sticky, greasy, salty, and sweet all at the same time.

I thought that only the people on River Ridge would eat such a thing, but I was wrong. In West Tennessee, I found potatoes made almost like Daddy's. The difference was they were covered in cayenne pepper. If you bought them, you had better get yourself a carton of buttermilk and a small container of cottage cheese, because you were going to need both. Another thing, you made sure that you went back to the office to go to the bathroom. Relieving oneself out in the tall grass could result in a grass fire. Trust me on this. Appalachian Boys just know stuff.

Here is what you need and how to do it:

- Wash about eight potatoes.
- Boil them until they are just about halfway cooked.
- Take them out of the water and let them cool.
- Turn the oven on to 400 degrees.
- When the oven is hot and the potatoes are cool, dry them off and cut them into quarters.
- Melt about one cup of lard in the very large cast-iron skillet.
- Roll the potato wedges in eggs, then in flour and then in cornmeal.
- Place the potato wedges in grease in the cast-iron skillet and roll them around so they don't stick.
- Add salt, to taste – that means a lot.
- Add black pepper, to taste – yes, that means a lot too.
- Red hot pepper, just a little. Daddy did not like hot peppers too much, but I do pour it to mine.
- Put them on a large, flat pan in the hot oven.
- Now, when the potatoes are about five minutes from being cooked, uniformly cover each potato wedge with Karo Syrup, the kind that comes in a metal can and is real thick. There is a picture of a big lion on the label.
- Bake until they are crispy-looking on the outside.

Serving suggestions:

You need a dish of fresh kale or turnip greens. Wild greens would be great if you can find them. The sour taste of vinegar is good with Karo Syrup. It might not be a bad idea to have some shelled October beans or a green bean casserole, and some real yellow chicken and dumplings would help the meal out, too. A large glass of sweet milk would be nice. No buttermilk, please; save that for when you are having cornbread. You don't need coffee unless you are eating supper.

Stuffed Peppers

One of the staples of every Lytton family reunion is stuffed peppers. A few family reunions I have attended have been graded, not on the number of people in attendance, but solely on the quantity and quality of the stuffed peppers. Some are going to tell you right off that Aunt Maud's were the best. While some will go to their grave telling you that Charlene Harris' were by far the best. There is even a group that will tell you the baked ones are far superior to the raw ones.

I am going to leave some of the research up to you. I have been working on the stuffed pepper recipe and this ongoing controversy for about 55 years now, with no end in sight.

I love to go to family reunions. My mother, Ruth, is committed to capturing "The Lytton Family Reunions." She is the picture-taker, which I think is good. She has never taken more than a half a dozen pictures of people. She only takes pictures of the food. In the last few years others have started taking pictures, too. Now, a few people attending get photographed.

Sometimes an older person will just show up and tell people: "I am your Uncle So-and-So's youngest son." It is always great to meet new family members or see those you've missed for four or five years. It is also fun to meet people who claim to kin, all the while knowing they just wanted to eat some stuffed peppers done the right way!

The second best thing is watching the family start eyeing the stuffed peppers. They just stand by and look them over. They are trying to figure out who has made each version and determine which one they are going eat first. Later you will hear comments like, "Them were Aunt Maude's. There is plate full of Charlene's. Them there are somebody's, don't know whose. I won't eat them first. They look like somebody is trying to copy out Aunt Maude or someone else."

Those last ones, most likely, are mine. They are slow to be eaten, but the plate is clean when I go home.

Hell, I have been known to eat a whole plate full of lesser quality peppers just as a way to offer encouragement -- you know, a way to keep family spirits high in the hope their stuffed-pepper-making skills improve before next year.

There are many guarded family secrets when it comes to stuffed peppers. This recipe will get you started off on the right foot.

I can promise that your grandmother will start to tell you everything that you did wrong with them peppers. She will do this while munching down on her eight or ninth pepper. Just keep a careful ear out for that one cherished family secret. It will come out soon! And, please, invite me, too.

Here is want you need:

- Ten solid fresh green peppers
- Salt and pepper
- Some red pepper
- A small shake of flour and dill weed
- Both red and white onions
- Louisiana Hot Sauce
- One pound of hamburger
- One pound of sausage
- One cucumber
- One red, one yellow and one pink tomato.
- One or two pounds of shredded sharp cheese
- Mayonnaise
- Bread crumbs
- Sweet corn is an option. Some stuffed peppers have corn; some do not.
- Momma Ruth always added two large cans of potted meat to hers -- gives them a little tang, just something to set them apart from the others, she says.

Now, here is what you do:

- Go to the garden and pick ten good solid peppers, free of any blemishes! Wash them and cut them in half long-ways, so they look like little boats.
- Pull seven or eight good solid onions, red and yellow, if you've got them.
- Brown the hamburger and sausage; add in salt and pepper and some Louisiana Hot Sauce; then add in about one cup of onion so that it can cook down.
- Drain off all the grease from the hamburger and the sausage.
- Make up about 4 cups of toasted breadcrumbs.
- When the meat has drained, put it in a large bowl with the remaining raw onion, about two pounds of shredded sharp cheese, salt, pepper, a few pieces of the raw tomato, a finely chopped cucumber and one cup of mayonnaise. Add more mayo if needed to hold the stuffing together. Add in about half of the breadcrumbs and then more as needed.

44

- Mix it up well and taste it; if it needs spices add them now – you know, those old family secrets.

- Put the mixture in the pepper halves and put them in the refrigerator overnight to age and set up (if they will last that long). Serve them cold.

Now, if you are of a mind to bake your stuffed pepper, it is okay. Daddy said that was the way people ate them in the city. Many of the steps are the same, but there are a few importance differences too.

- Go to the garden and pick ten good solid peppers free of any blemishes! Wash them.
- Pull seven or eight good solid onions, red and yellow if you have them.
- One red, one yellow and pink tomato
- Brown one or more pounds of hamburger and sausage, add in salt and pepper and some Louisiana Hot Sauce.
- Also add in about one cup of onion so that it can cook down.
- Drain off all the grease from the hamburger and the sausage.
- Cut the tops of the peppers off. And make sure that they will stand up in your baking pan
- In a big mixing bowl combine all the meats, remaining raw onion, toasted breadcrumbs and about any leftovers you have in the refrigerator, about two pounds of shredded sharp cheese, salt, pepper, a few pieces of the raw tomato, a finely chopped cucumber, yellow squash and two raw eggs.
- Mix it up well and fill the empty peppers, and put them in the oven for 30 minutes at 400 degrees or until the egg is done.
- Drain and serve.

Scalded Lettuce

We ate a lot of green things! "You need it to go with pinto beans and cracklin bread," Elmer would say.

In the spring we ate every kind of wild greens that could be located. Soon spinach, kale and mustard would appear in the garden. They supplemented the wild green diet.

In late spring everyone's attention turned to "scalded lettuce." We ate scalded lettuce for every supper until it was gone. Except on weekends that is; on Saturday and Sunday we ate scalded lettuce for both lunch and supper.

Yes, we were eating cabbage, boiled cabbage, cabbage rolls, fried cabbage and cold slaw. Fried cabbage accompanied about every meal until sauerkraut and chowchow time. Then we started on the turnip greens.

There are many recipes for each dish, most of which were just dreamed up on the spot. Yes sir, we had sound digestive systems no doubt about it. But the crème de la crème of spring greens is none other than scalded lettuce! Now, if you want to do it right, just follow the short recipe on the next page.

46

Here is what you need:

- One pound of streaky salt-cured bacon
- A large deep skillet or deep roasting pan; one that will hold two gallons or more. You do not want stuff to come out when you pour in the cold vinegar.
- A very large bowl, again something that will hold upwards on two gallons
- A cup of apple cider vinegar
- Pepper and maybe salt (Season to your own taste.)
- Seven or eight fresh green onions with the tops still on
- A brown grocery bag full of fresh leaf lettuce -- a little extra just in case.

Now, here is what you do:

- Wash the onions, cut them into pieces about 1/2" long and put them a bowl.
- Wash and drain the lettuce and put it in the bowl, too.
- Cut the bacon into small pieces about one inch long. If it is real salty, you may wash it off and drain it good and dry.
- Fry the bacon real slow to render all the pork fat out.
- Look at the bacon fat. If there is more in the pan than you think you need, dip out some for another day.
- Put the lettuce, bacon pieces and onions in the largest bowl you have. Mix them up a little.
- Pour the vinegar into the grease and try not to get burned. Be mindful of eyes and nose. It is going to be real tight for a moment or two.
- Now, pour the vinegar and grease over the lettuce and onions.
- With a big spoon mix it around a few times and serve.

Serving suggestions:

I recommend that you serve cornbread, cow butter and sweet tea with your scalded lettuce. That is all that is needed. Serve pinto beans, too, if you have them, but they are not truly needed. The scalded lettuce is so good people sometimes forget to eat their beans.

47

Eating the Bait and Fried Green Tomatoes

In the spring, one day you find that you have just set around the house about all you can. When this happened to us, we came up with a plan for going fishing. It was very cold; the pond was not frozen over but it could freeze if it wanted too.

Because the ground was too hard for digging worms, I settled in on making dough balls. The only problem was we had never made such a thing. So I got out the flour can and went to adding water, sugar, salt and lard. I mixed up something that looked like it would stay on a hook and headed for the river. The fish hated them, plus they would not stay on the hook very well, and I was getting hungry. Whose idea was this anyway, I was thinking. So I dug around in the weeds and found the cast-iron gigging skillet.

I scrubbed out the rust with sand and washed it in the river. I built up a right small driftwood fire on the riverbank, and when it turned to ash I set the skillet on the fire and dropped in some dough balls. They looked kind of like a poorly fried biscuit. They were about the worst-tasting things. I wish that I had not eaten seven or eight. You talk about something that needed yellow cow butter! A little salt would not have hurt either, and I really wished for some milk and jelly.

Another fine fish bait that I have eaten is chicken livers. Now, there is nothing wrong with chicken livers. In fact, I like them. Sometimes today I will buy a pint of them to cook. They are great with bacon and a little spicy mustard. A well-fried chicken liver fits just right on top of a biscuit.

One late spring when the fishing fever hit again, I brought home two quarts of chicken livers. It was cool, so I just left them in the back of the truck for the night. The next day I headed for the river.

I paddled over to the Whiterock Hole and dropped anchor. It was just a short ways. I sat there until late afternoon and never got one bite. I was getting very hungry. The warm spring sun and cool river breezes will do you that way. So I paddled to the bus (our fishing headquarters), and there was nothing there to eat. There was not a cracker, not a can of sardines, not even potted meat.

I was getting desperate. I went back to the boat and dug out five or six of the cleanest-looking chicken livers. Keep in mind that they had been out of refrigeration for more than 36 hours and in the warm sun for six or seven hours. I pitched them into the river to wash them off, then I left them to dry off on a big orange flint rock. I started a fire in the warming stove in the cabin and spooned in a big dollop of Crisco. I lay them livers in the grease, and when they turned dark brown I dug them out and ate them.

They were right good. I think they had every opportunity to be full of botulism or something really bad. But they weren't. I never even got as much as a stomach ache. The stomach of an Appalachian male is truly a wonder of mankind!

Another time we had made up a plan to go to my friend's grandfather's farm and put out a few trotlines. We were going to use crawfish for bait. They make great bait. We started turning over rocks and catching the little hellions. It was slow going. Then my friend came over the hill with his Farmall Super "C" International Tractor and drove it up the creek a few times until the water got real muddy. We pulled a seine up through the muddy water and caught enough crawfish for the night.

Since we had a 30-gallon trash can full of bait, we took off quickly for Pembroke. By the time we arrived, we learned that it had rained upstream or something. Anyway the dam had discharged lots of water. The river was too full to put out the trotlines, so we got right down to drinking beer.

After a while we got awful hungry. We decided that we were going to boil the crawfish and eat them. We built up a very big fire and set the trashcan on the fire. It took the trashcan at least two hours to come close to boiling. The more beer we drank the more done those crawfish looked. We ate them and enjoyed yet another cold Blue Ribbon beer. The cooking water never came close to boiling. No one even came close to being sick as I recall. Some might have been sick, but I do think it was the Blue Ribbon not the crawfish.

Today, I am not eating crawfish unless they are washed off some and truly cooked in boiling water. As I look back, I figure those crawfish that were mostly warm all the way through were a little chewier than I liked!

Here is another dose of my Appalachian cuisine. It was very late fall and I was fooling around on the river. Usually when doing this, you go to the garden and pick some tomatoes, a roasting ear, a pepper or a cantaloupe. In this case the garden had been cleaned out weeks before to make chowchow. It was late in the day, and I was getting hungrier all the time. I looked the garden over, and all I could find was a few green tomatoes that were covered up by tall weeds. I picked them and headed for the bus.

On the stove I found the old cast-iron skillet half-full of old sausage grease. Keep in mind -- I left it that way so it would not rust. The leftover grease in the pan was no more than two weeks old. I built a fire. While the fire was catching up, I took a knife and scooped out all of the small mouse footprints in the grease. I was thinking that if I let the grease boil for a minute it would kill the germs.

So, I did indeed let the pan boil for a minute or two and then put the green tomatoes in to fry. In a minute I took them out, and they looked mighty good. But, right from the start they tasted awful. I even poured ketchup on them to give them a ripe taste. They still tasted real bad, very bad.

Well, I just started for home. I had walked about 15 minutes up the path from the bus. When I was up about to the pond, I started to cramp up badly and vomit very badly. My other end was real active as well.

It seemed like it took hours to get home. Mother Ruth just shook her head. "One of these days you are going to do something that is going to give you rabies or kill you or something worse. Just you mark my words." Elmer just shook his head and chuckled under his breath.

For about a day I thought I would just die. I think the ketchup was old or something. I still like fried green tomatoes, but now I am very careful with the ketchup!

Truly, every few weeks through the summer someone will ask me how you make fried green tomatoes. Well, this is how I do it.

Here is what you need:

- Get about five or six good solid green tomatoes, no red or yellow on them
- One full cup of flour
- One full cup of cornmeal
- At least a cup of lard; Crisco will do if you don't have lard.
- One tablespoon of salt and black pepper
- 1/2 tablespoon of basil and oregano (no rosemary; it is too strong)
- Two cups of milk and two eggs

Now, here is what you do:

- Mix the flour and cornmeal in a bowl.
- Add in the salt, pepper and basil and oregano (more or less depending on how you like it).
- Get the grease hot in your big cast-iron skillet. You want the tomato to sizzle when it is put into the grease.
- Popcorn for testing (When the popcorn pops, the lard has reached the proper temperature for cooking.)
- Mix the eggs and milk in a deep bowl.
- Roll the tomato in the milk and eggs.
- Roll it in the flour/cornmeal/salt/pepper/herb mixture.
- Lay the tomato into the hot grease; make sure that you do not get burned, but try to move the tomato quickly to keep it from sticking.
- Slide the tomatoes around in the pan one time, and then turn them over. They are done when golden brown on both sides.
-

Serving suggestions:

As children we ate fried green tomatoes for breakfast. Mom always served them with hot biscuits, butter, hot salt-cured bacon, fried eggs, coffee and sweet milk. If you wish, you can make tomato gravy out of the stuff left in the tomato pan. Just let it cool a little and add in your leftover milk, eggs and flour. Bring it to a low boil and let it simmer. Just make sure you stir it a lot so it doesn't get lumpy. It is hard for an Appalachian American to eat lumpy gravy of any kind. It is not so hard on your teeth. It's hard on your pride. Lumpy gravy is for town boys.

Spaghetti, the Way Grandmother Never Made It

Have I told you that I love spaghetti? During the summer, about every week or two we had spaghetti and a lot of it. We Lyttons have big appetites and there are a lot of us. Never once did my Mom ever think of making foods measured in servings. Momma measured things in gallons.

When I was little -- no when I was younger, I never was little -- my mother and grandmother would make somewhere in the neighborhood of two gallons of spaghetti. Yes, I liked it. Momma's recipe was simple: one quart of water, five or six pounds of hamburger, a peck of red tomatoes and eight or ten bell peppers from the garden. Add two or three boxes of spaghetti with salt, black pepper and garlic. She would let it boil for a while and then it was suppertime.

Today my recipe is a little different from Mother's and Grandmother's. Also, it will help a lot if you are into growing fresh herbs. Me, I always have flower pots just out my back door.

Here is what you need:

- 1/2 box of whole-wheat spaghetti
- One very large onion – chopped
- Four or five tablespoons of minced garlic
- A handful -- each --of fresh thyme, rosemary, basil, chives, and parsley
- One 10 ounce bag of fresh spinach
- One 16 ounce can of chopped tomatoes (fresh ones are okay too)
- One cup of mayonnaise
- 1/2 cup of olive oil
- 1/2 cup parmesan cheese
- Salt and pepper
- A big spaghetti pan and a big cast-iron skillet

Now here is what you do:

- Pour about two quarts of cold water into your big spaghetti pan.
- Dump in the one cup of mayonnaise. Turn the stove eye on medium heat. If you heat up the water too fast the mayonnaise will form lumps. If it does, that's okay. It may just add a little more character to the overall dish.
- Add in one tablespoon of salt.
- Once the water is good and hot, turn up the heat to high. When it is boiling, add in the spaghetti. Cook until done –to the texture you like.
- In the cold cast-iron skillet add the olive oil and onion. Cook on low heat until the onion is clear.
- Add the garlic and keep the heat on low.
- Add the rosemary, thyme, parsley and basil. Now onto the chives.
- Once the herbs have cooked for about three minutes on low, add the can of tomatoes.
- Do not turn up the heat, but when the sauce is again hot add the bag of spinach. Now turn off the heat.
- Drain the spaghetti. When the spinach has wilted, dump the spaghetti into the cast-iron skillet.
- Dump the spaghetti and sauce into a serving platter, dust with parmesan cheese and garnish with olives.

Serving suggestions:

I like to serve this dish with a glass of dry rosé.

I also like a large tossed salad made with romaine lettuce, fresh oranges, green onions and large pieces of fresh parmesan cheese.

I also like little cherry tomatoes scalded in olive oil, salt pepper, rosemary, parsley and thyme. They need to be cooked only until the skins roll up some. Oh, once in a while I will live a little on the wild side and add in one or two very small green tomatoes. They add a little green color and tartness.

THE MEAT
OF
THE MATTER

Hog Killing and Fresh Liver

Thanksgiving Day was the target date for all hog killing. I truly never had a traditional Thanksgiving meal until I was grown and cooked it. We killed hogs!! But about dark we did eat fresh pork liver and onions. It did not matter if it was raining, snowing, below zero or a hot Indian Summer day. If you had the flu or the whooping cough, you just had to get over it. You killed hogs and that was all there was to it!

Preparations started the week before with gathering up knives and gambling sticks, cleaning out the scalding barrel and refilling it with water, and building a small mountain of wood -- anything that you thought would burn would do. Everyone's smokehouse had to be cleaned, the meat tables washed and a thin layer of salt put down. At home, the sausage grinder was cleaned, the blade sharpened, lots of big pots and pans found. Someone had to go buy salt and Morton's Sausage Seasoning and lots of pepper, sugar and sage. Also, someone had to find all of the hog killing tools from last year -- things like head scrapers and snoot hooks. The first thing was to go in search of tools that were pitched down somewhere last year. Looking for a tool was a lot like looking for a lost ball in the high weeds.

59

A fire was built under the scalding barrel no later than 4:00 am. Well before daylight the men took to arguing about the temperature of the water, while everyone else went in all directions looking for equipment. It is a fact that if the water was too cool the hair would not turn loose from the skin, and you would have to almost shave the hog with a razor-sharp knife. If the water was too hot the hair would set -- with the same result. It seemed almost to cook into the pigskin.

I think that the water needs to be heated to about 160 degrees. The way you know it has reached the correct temperature is you drag a finger through the hot water three times. If you ain't got the nerve to drag your finger a fourth time, it is ready.

In my early life I was strictly a drag man, scald man and a hair puller. I was not given a knife ever. Daddy did not want to make things any easier than he had to. As Uncle Nelson would say, "You got a strong back and a weak mind."

I thought my heart would burst dragging the big hogs up the hill. The wood smoke and steam made me almost sick. I'd get right jumpy from the constant cuts and nicks you could get on your hands from drunks wielding razor-sharp knives.

I could not wait until I was old enough to graduate to head hair-puller or a boss at the scalding barrel. I would have my own knife then, I thought. For now, I just had to get the hog to the barrel, stick him in headfirst and work until the hair came loose. You pulled hair furiously standing in the wood smoke from the fire and being choked by the steam. For a little extra drama, you could do this job in a cold steady rain or a snowstorm. When the skin got cool, you shaved the rascal with a knife as sharp as any straight razor you ever saw.

Once a hog was scraped clean, it had to be lifted onto a scaffold, sometimes as much as eight to ten feet up into the air. Lifting the hog was called "the gambrel process." First you made a deep cut into the hog's heels, thus exposing the large tendons. A three- foot-long stick was placed behind these tendons. The stick carried the weight of the hog once it was lifted to the scaffold pole.

We carried the big hogs to the bottom of an inclined pole, completed the gambling process and as a group slid them up onto the scaffold. Holy Macaroni they were heavy!

Now, the men required a celebratory drink while my brothers and friends and I started the next hog. Then, Uncle Shorty gutted the hog and left it to cool out.

One of the saddest parts of the job was rationalizing the hog into products like ham, sausage, fried liver and so on. You had to sometimes just keep thinking it over and over. "I like pork, I like Boston Butts and I like sausage" --- just keep saying it over and over. Sometimes I think that we grew up quick and real early. Not many grownups have ever had to do anything like butcher hogs, but this was the rural way.

Young men were bonded for life by pure, raw physical strength, strong stomachs and willing hearts. The true

Appalachian Tradition lives through us. Yes, I was big, and I was strong and I could lift with the best of them. I took pride in being able to lift my half of a 400-pound hog. But, it was a very happy time when I graduated to Chief Hog Gutting Specialist. That got me away from the big razor-sharp knives.

After a hard day of hog-killing, the first meal we all enjoyed was fresh liver and onions. Some of the time, when the liver was fixed it was still warm with animal body heat. All local redneck boys ate and enjoyed it. The town boys that came along to watch and help, why they just set back and looked at that liver like it was something else, or maybe from Mars or something. We looked at it as great.

The day after Thanksgiving was spent cutting up the hogs. Hams were trimmed and salted. Tenderloin was cut out. Roasts were put into the freezer. Every scrap of meat was piled up and covered with Morton's Sausage Seasoning, lots of sage and black pepper. It was good!!!!

After we were about seven or eight years old we never thought of hogs as anything but meat. On the River Ridge hogs went from living animals to the human plate in a matter of hours. In town I think it took a little longer.

It is still this way. I know two little boys down the road with two hogs. One is named Pork, and the other is Chops. Both boys water and feed them each day. Their daddy says they have got to learn about the real world some day.

Here is what you need:

- A large cast-iron skillet
- Ten slices of salt-cured bacon fried real slow; keep all the bacon grease
- About two pounds of fresh liver cut into ½-inch slices
- Give or take five big onions, sliced and then diced up into large 1/2-inch pieces
- Flour
- A half gallon of cream. (Mom says she used more like a gallon of fresh milk. You kind of be the judge.)
- Salt and pepper

Now, here is what you do:

- Wash and drain each slice of liver.
- Roll each slice in flour and put it in the hot bacon grease, still in the pan you just fried the bacon in.
- Once you have all the liver in the pan, add in the onions. Salt and pepper to taste
- Fry the liver until it is done. Cut a piece if you have to. Cook only until all the pink is gone. DO NOT OVERCOOK THE LIVER.
- Dip out the liver slices and set them in the warming oven.
- Let the cast-iron skillet cool down to warm.
- Add in a cup of all-purpose flour (In some families you may need more flour; you be the judge.)
- Put the pan back on the heat. Take a spatula and scrape up all the small liver pieces, onions and flour that have cooked to the bottom of the pan.
- Stir and scrape until all the flour is worked into the pan leavings.
- Pour in somewhere between a quart and ½ gallon of cream and slowly bring the gravy up to a low boil.
- Cut the heat way down and let the gravy simmer for 10 minutes. Taste for salt and pepper. Now it is ready to serve.

Serving suggestions:

I think the best combination is a pan of fresh cornbread, yellow cow butter, cold sweet milk, and turnip greens with pieces of turnip cooked in the greens. Butter the cornbread as soon as it comes from the pan. Put a piece of liver on the plate with a piece of cornbread that you cover with gravy. Dice up onions in the greens and serve them in a bowl with lots of black pepper and vinegar.

A good quart of thick buttermilk is so good with liver and onions that it will let you forget for a while the work yet to be done today.

Pig's Feet for the Gigging Boys

One time, we were gigging just after Thanksgiving. Everybody killed hogs at Thanksgiving. We had a big cooking fire going for when someone showed up with fresh pig's feet. I was sent to the weeds to get the sliding board, our cooktop. The old pans were cleaned, and the pig's feet put on to boil. The cast-iron skillet was shined and put on the sliding board with a great big dollop of last year's lard melting in it.

We chopped each pig's foot right down the middle with an ax. Some had already been sawed in two. Each half was rolled in flour and very carefully placed in the grease. If you dropped one you could set the world on fire or burn one of your hands off up to the elbow. The feet cooked a minute or two on each side until they got right brown. Then they were set on the bucket lid.

There was no serving dishes used when you were gigging. There's a rule when gigging against any extra dishes. Most of the time you just got the hot stuff out of the pan and somehow held onto it until you worked up the nerve to stick it in your mouth.

For me, hog's feet always fell into a category all their own. I had to work up the nerve to start on mine. It was right tough; there was no meat to speak of. After you had fought your way through the skin and leftover hair there wasn't much else. Everyone seemed to just love them.

Thinking back, I guess I did like them too. I guess anything cooked late at night over an open fire in the cool night air is always good. Throw in an air-cooled Blue Ribbon or two. Just never you mind the grit, dirt, burnt tough bone, gristle, fat, salt and wood ashes.

There are lots of ways to fix pig's feet. For example, you can fry them, or you can bake them. Some people even cook them in sauerkraut. Pig's feet are the kind of food that you did not tell people you ate. They are considered a by-product from hog killing, in the same classification as chitlins.

Eating pig's feet will do nothing for your social standing in the community. We ate them mostly on the river while gigging so no one could see us doing it.

I have also eaten pickled pig's feet from a jar. My alcoholic mentors would eat them like there was no tomorrow. They just dug them out of the jar with their fingers and started eating. I ate them only once, and they made me a little sick. I think it was that sour-tasting jelly and rotten-smelling cartilage that did me in.

Here is what you need:

- It is best to have pig's feet from either white or red hogs. They tend to be easier to clean up than the feet from black hogs.
- With a razor-sharp pocketknife, shave the last bits of hair from the pig's feet.
- Cut them in half if you can. You may need a meat saw. An old hand saw is what we mostly used.
- Wash them right good for the second time.
- Three eggs
- Two cups of flour
- A can of sage (herb)
- Salt and pepper
- Cayenne pepper

Now here is what you do:

- Put them on to parboil for a while. Boil them until they are about tender.
- Heat up a big cast-iron skillet with about a cup of lard. Crisco will do in a pinch.
- Take them out of the hot water and let them cool until you can handle them. If you don't you are going to get scalded when the water drops in the hot lard.
- Roll them in eggs and then in flour.
- Very gently lay them in the skillet, the carefuller the better.
- Sprinkle with salt and pepper to taste; dust with sage. Also, some like them with red cayenne pepper.
- Cook until they are crispy and brown. They will never get tender, but they will get brown.
- Remember, they are a little thick, so cook them a little slower.

Serving suggestions:

At home you can serve pig's feet with fried potatoes, well-drained and washed fried sauerkraut, and two-day-old pinto beans. Cornbread if you've got it. Just don't be telling people that you ate them. We Lyttons have a very stalwart reputation to keep up, you know.

Now, if you are gigging have lots of beer with them, too. I would suggest that you drink some of the beer first. This may speed up your digestion. If you are eating them at home, milk and tomato juice is recommended.

A good sour apple pie is good, too, with fresh whipped cream on top. And strong coffee with some of that fresh cream is just plain good.

Fried Hog Brains

Another food item that falls into the "needs to be experienced category" is hog brains. Uncle Shorty gave me my first lesson on hog brains, and I ain't forgotten it yet. One morning we had extracted the brains from five hogsheads. We took them in the house. Mamaw had made fresh hot coffee and biscuits.

There were always fried pies around. I could have eaten the pies and been real happy. But no, Shorty washed brains —two to three sets of brains—set them aside and put some just-made lard in a small cast-iron skillet on the wood cook stove. While the grease got to bubbling, he took a half a dozen eggs and beat them into scrambled eggs. He set them brains in the hot grease and they went to sizzling real fast. Since it was lunchtime he added onion pieces. For Shorty, onions were part of every lunch. Raw, fried or green, he ate onions.

Well, the eggs were poured in as quickly as the brains were turned over. When the eggs stopped being runny, the brains and eggs were done. Shorty took to eating; he liked it a lot. Grandmother said that if I (Charles) was going to eat any, she thought we ought to at least make sure they were warm all the way through. I ate the eggs and brains she fixed. I just could not eat the cool, runny ones. The hot biscuits with yellow cow butter were the best part of eggs and brains.

Stuffed Veal

About every spring Daddy would come home with three or four bottle calves from the Adams' Farm. He always told us right from the start that these were going to be veal calves. At six or seven years old I did not know what this meant. I just guessed that was their names. Yes, all of them were named Veal. But anyway I didn't know what was going to happen.

Just like it was with most everything else on the place, one day Mr. Henry Lee Curtis showed up. Into his truck, we loaded up the calves and he hauled them off. Then in a few days Daddy would bring in another set of new baby calves.

We would clean out their little stalls in the barn and put in fresh clean dirt and cover it with hay for bedding. The stalls were so small that the calves could barely turn around, and as they got bigger they could not turn around. When I asked why, the answer was, "You see them calves don't have any other place to go."

It sounded reasonable to me. A calf doesn't have many places it can go, and the barn seemed okay with me. Every day, I just bottle-fed them all of the fresh milk we did not drink. Me and the calves grew fat together. I talked to them and scratched their backs and heads, and they stuck out their tongues and sucked my finger.

Then one day the biggest calf was gone. Mr. Henry Lee Curtis' truck had not been to the barn. This time when I asked about him, they said that he had found a much better place to go. That night for supper we had a special dish. Something that Mom truly loved: "Stuffed Veal," she called it.

I soon learned that life was full of lessons. The fate of my baby calf was a hard one.

Here is what you need:

- Veal loin with the chops and ribs attached
- Strips of salt pork
- A large cast-iron Dutch oven with a little shelf in it to keep the veal off the bottom
- Garlic salt
- Salt and pepper
- Cornbread crumbs

Now, here is what you do:

- Set the oven on 450 degrees.
- On the outside of the rib cut along the bone all the way to the backbone, forming a pocket between the ribs and the loin.
- Recipe for dressing: two pieces of cold cornbread, one egg, a sprinkle of sage, 1/4 tablespoon of salt, 1/4 teaspoon of black pepper, one cup of celery chopped very small, one onion from the garden chopped the same size as the celery. Mix the stuffing up in a bowl until it is well stuck together.
- Pack the cavity created along the rib full of stuffing.
- Rub the outside of the loin with a very thin layer of lard. Roll the loin in cornbread crumbs.
- Cover the outside of the loin with strips of salt-cured bacon. (In more modern times I have used bacon from the grocery store to reduce the salt. It works just as well.)
- Sprinkle with garlic salt.
- Place in the Dutch oven, rib side down, on the little rack.
- Bake for one hour or until done.

Real Deer Meat Chili

In early 1960 I was sitting on top of the Whiterock and looked across the river to the rock bar. There stood the first deer I'd ever seen. I had heard the grownups talk about deer being stocked in the Radford Arsenal. By damn, there stood one. When I told Daddy, he accused me of being a bald-faced liar. I had to paddle him across the river, with Mod, Shorty and Gilbert standing on the bank, to see the animals' tracks.

Yes, there they were. So my deer story was right after all. I have always heard about people and families that communicated and believed in one another. Not on River Ridge, no matter what. I was a liar until proven otherwise. Daddy never once said, "You were right after all, and I was wrong."

Within a few years the novelty wore off. Those rascals became a nuisance. They ate up gardens and the flowers out of the yard, and were always running into cars. Well, we ate them too; so I guess we got even. We ate chicken-fried deer steak; now that is real good. Sometimes we had venison ground up into burgers and put it on pizza; some liked that, too. But, the best way to eat deer meat is in chili. Here is how we made it. Go hunting and catch a big one and give it a try.

Here is what you need:

- One 16-ounce bag of dry kidney beans. This may sound like a lot, but there was a lot of us to feed.
- About three ounces of cooking oil – lard will work, too.
- Six pounds of deer meat, made into hamburger.
- At least three large onions, more if you like onions.
- Four large garlic cloves
- Two big green sweet peppers
- At least one large green chili pepper. If you do not have a green chili pepper, you can use a jalapeno. But be careful, some jalapenos are real hot. You can just use the kind that comes in a can, too.
- One big can of whole tomatoes. You can get them from the garden in the summer.
- One can of real thick tomato juice or crushed tomatoes.
- Some water??
- Two or three teaspoons of cayenne pepper. You be the judge about how hot you like it.
- Two tablespoons of cumin. I like the cumin; keep it handy; you might want a little more later.
- One big dash of Worchester sauce
- Salt, black pepper and red pepper to your taste
- A cup of cold coffee
- Here is my secret ingredient -- a couple squares of bitter chocolate.

Now, here is what you do:

- Wash and soak the beans overnight. Cook them in the large Dutch oven until almost done and let them cool.
- Heat up the oven to 300 degrees.
- In a really large cast-iron pan, brown the venison, then cook the onion, garlic and peppers until tender.
- Add in a tablespoon cayenne pepper to your taste, 1/2 tablespoon of black pepper, a tablespoon of cumin and a tablespoon of salt. Then stir for about two minutes on low heat.

- Pour all of the tomatoes and hot peppers into the bean pot. If it is a little dry looking, add in about a cup of water.

- Add in the coffee and the chocolate, but to make sure the chocolate melts, keep on stirring. If the chocolate is in a hard block, you can shred it a little.

- Take out a few spoonfuls and let it cool down and taste it; then adjust spices.

- Put the mixture in the oven for at least 90 minutes -- or until the beans are tender.

Serving Suggestions:

I would suggest having a bowl of green onions chopped up and setting on the dining room table. Chop the tops and all. I also like to have fresh green peppers, too. If you have the sweet red bell pepper, they are good. Sour cream is also recommended.

Now, it is important to have fresh, hot cracklin cornbread with lots of yellow cow butter.

One of my best recommendations is to have plenty of real cold buttermilk on hand, because you are going to need it.

In the fall there will be lots of fresh cabbage for coleslaw, too. A dish of fried turnips would be most welcome. It is always good.

Corned Beef Hash or Corned Beef Gravy

I love corned beef gravy! I know what you are thinking: "Why in the world did that boy add in a whole section about some kind of gravy?" Well, it is not just gravy; it is corned beef hash. Hash was an important part of my growing up on River Ridge. I thought that it kept me alive; now as I look toward my shoes I see that it may be more on the order of the death of me.

We had it for breakfast, lunch or supper. When I was younger I thought we ate it because we all liked it so much. Later I learned we ate it because we had to. It was really cheap to make. There was nothing much else in the house until payday. Sometimes we ate corned beef hash when Mom and Dad got tired of salt pork for breakfast, too. Thank goodness for paydays and corned beef hash. Today, I eat this just because I love the stuff. Just reading the recipes -- I've included one for both kinds we ate -- may clog up your blood veins.

Here is what you need.

- A two-gallon stew pot
- Two cans of corned beef (You may only need one or you may need three, you be the judge of your crowd, ok?)
- A few strips of salt pork bacon (this is optional). If you don't want to use your bacon, a cup of lard will do.
- Three big onions
- Butter. I am guessing about two cups.
- A cup or so of flour
- Salt and pepper
- Three quarts of sweet milk if you got it. If not, water will do in a bind.
- One quart of water.

Now, here is what you do.

Mom and Grandmother never measured anything. They just knew how much stuff to pitch in the pan. So, please just use this a guide as you work toward "Corned Beef Hash" perfection.

- Fry the bacon and hold onto the bacon drippings. (You can go on and eat the bacon while the corned beef hash is cooking.)
- Put a cup of fresh cow butter in the big pan with bacon grease to melt.
- Chop up all the onions and put them in the butter to cook. Cook only until they are starting to get clear.
- Add in one can of corned beef (two if you need it). With a potato masher, mash up the corned beef and stir it around until each strand of beef has been separated. Fry everything for a minute or two. Add in more butter if you like. (I suggest you add the butter.)
- Add in one quart of water and let the mixture come to a good boil. Then let the pan cool down.
- In a big bowl add the milk, one cup of flour, 1/2 teaspoon of salt and one tablespoon of pepper. Mix this with a fork until there are no lumps. Add in a little more milk if you need to. You want this to be like a thin paste.
- Slowly pour the paste into the cool pan. Never stop stirring -- not even for a second. Once the stuff is thoroughly mixed turn up the heat and bring it to a low boil. Make sure to keep mixing.

- Let the hash boil for a few minutes, then cool down. When it is mostly cool you can see how thick it is going to be. The goal is to have it thick enough that a spoon will stand up in the pan. You may have to play with the recipe a little to get the exact ratios of ingredients for your taste. And, be aware – the milk will stick.

Serving suggestions:

Now, how do you serve corned beef hash the correct way? For breakfast, you need two large cat-headed biscuits cut open with fresh yellow cow butter added. Close the biscuits and turn them up on their tops until the butter melts. When you open up the biscuits add a slice of fresh, dead-ripe, red tomato to each biscuit. Then spoon about one cup of hash onto each. It is ok to add eggs, too, if you have them. Cold sweet milk is advised. Homemade jelly is good too. Strong coffee is always welcome.

For supper, corned beef hash is good with fresh greens and cornbread. Sweet milk is a welcome addition. If you are eating this for lunch or for supper, a tall glass of sweet tea is a good idea.

• • #2 • •

Here is what you need:

- The big Dutch oven
- Eight right large potatoes, washed and cut into very small cubes
- Eight whole onions from the garden, tops and all, cut into the same size pieces as the potatoes
- Eight or ten carrots, if you can dig them up. (If you can't that is ok.) Cut them into the same size pieces as the potatoes.
- A full cup of yellow cow butter
- About one quart of sweet cream
- The kernels cut off six or eight ears of sweet corn
- Four slices of salt-cured bacon
- Two large cans of corned beef
- One quart water
- Salt and pepper

79

Now, here is what you do:

- In a right large Dutch oven, fry the bacon until it is crispy. Then take it out, break it into little pieces and set it aside.
- Add the corned beef to the bacon drippings (Drippings sounds better than bacon grease, don't it?) and stir it around until it is separated into individual pieces of meat.
- Add in the potatoes, carrots and onions.
- Add just enough water to cover the mixture.
- Add in some salt and pepper to taste. Remember the salt-cured bacon, and go light on the salt
- Now add in the corn, cut back on the heat and let the mixture come to a very low boil. Taste for your salt and pepper again
- Move the Dutch oven to a less hot side of the stove. Add in the sweet cream and let the hash cook real slow. Keep in mind that it will stick very easily, so you might have to stir it some.
- Cook until the potatoes are tender.
- If the hash does not get as thick as you like, you can add in a little flour paste.
- When you serve the hash, crumble the bacon back on top.

Serving suggestions:

For the most part this was served at suppertime. I always like good fresh greens of any kind with mine. Sometimes there were no fresh greens and Mom would have to open a can of the greens we had put up during the spring and summer.

Cornbread is good, too. Strong sweet tea is welcome. Yes, corned beef hash, greens, sweet tea and cornbread.

Squirrels

Squirrel hunting was just part of growing up on River Ridge. I did it for entertainment and for food. I just loved the woods and the trees. I could sit for hours and enjoy the cool breezes. Sometimes I would start out very early in the morning before the sun came up. I'd find a most comfortable seat beside a large hickory and settle back and wait for daylight, only to be aroused by the bright sun glaring in my eyes. Yes, I fell asleep again and did no hunting.

Another treat was fried squirrel and squirrel gravy. Around River Ridge so many stories had been told about squirrel hunting and squirrel gravy that my little niece, Rebecca, then eight years old, wanted to go hunting and to eat a squirrel. Rebecca is from Indianapolis, Indiana. She has been for a walk or two around the woods in her town, but rarely has she ever ventured into the deep woods on River Ridge. Oh, Rebecca is a real picky eater. In the past I had observed her eating macaroni and few other things, but never squirrel.

One day, we head for the closet at Mother's and take out Daddy's old 12-gauge and walk over the hill into the woods. We find ourselves a comfortable seat and start concentrating on being quiet. Little Rebecca draws real close to me and I think, "This is wonderful. My favorite niece and me squirrel-hunting together. Life is good."

After a few minutes, a nice, big, fat-looking squirrel goes running down a limb of a fine hickory tree. I look at Rebecca to see if she is still thinking serious about shooting the small rodent. She gives me a look of approval.

Boom! The 12-gauge roars to life and the squirrel falls out of the tree and rolls far down over the hill. Little Rebecca charges down after her trophy. After a while she drags herself and the squirrel back to our seat. She lays him down on the ground at our feet and we sit and talk about our victorious hunt. "He is a fine squirrel, isn't he?" we agree.

She picks up the dead squirrel and heads off home to show him to her grandfather. In just a few minutes she comes running and pitches the squirrel on the ground right at my feet. "I forgot to tell you I am scared to death of this thing. I did not remember until I got to Granddaddy's house. I did not know what to do, so I brought the thing back to you."

We dig around in the trash dump and find her an old mayonnaise jar to carry the squirrel in. Back up over the hill she goes again.

After a while we butcher the squirrel and review his anatomy. Next Rebecca puts him in the refrigerator in a pan of cold saltwater to soak for a while. We wash up and set down for that same while. We soon realize it's near suppertime, so we go to one of the popular local restaurants, where nice, handsome young men and very pretty young ladies work. You can tell that not one of them is a true squirrel-hunter like Rebecca and me.

One of the very nice young ladies comes to our table. Rebecca says, "Well, I do not want much. You see, I left Granddaddy at home to parboil my squirrel, and when I get home I am going to fry him and make a pan of gravy. So I don't want much."

The waitress just stares at Rebecca and then turns her gaze to us. "You are going to do what and eat what!!"

Rebecca says, "I thought everyone ate squirrels."

"Me, too," I say.

Here is what you need:

- Three or four squirrels cleaned, cut up, and soaking in cold saltwater. Why the saltwater? I do not know you just do this.
- One dish of flour
- Salt and pepper
- A cast-iron skillet
- Sweet milk
- Lard
- Thick cream

Now, here is what you do:

- Parboil the squirrel for about five minutes – save the water.
- Put the cast-iron skillet on the stove and heat up your lard. Test the temperature with popcorn.
- Dry off all the pieces of the squirrel.
- Roll the squirrel in a dish of milk, and then roll the meat in the dish of flour.
- You do not want your squirrel to taste greasy, so make sure the lard is hot enough that all three or four pieces of popcorn have popped.
- Slowly lay the meat in the hot lard.
- Fill the pan; add salt and pepper to taste.
- Try to only turn the squirrel one time.
- When it's golden brown, set the squirrel in a dish and set it in the warming oven.

Here's what you do for the gravy:

- Squirrel gravy is by far the most important kind of gravy there is for a country boy.
- After all the squirrel is cooked, dump about 3/4 cup of flour into the pan. More flour can be used if there is a lot of liquid and partly cooked flour.
- Take a stiff spatula and scrape all of the stuff stuck on the bottom of the pan; keep on moving the flour and cooked stuff.

- Once the flour absorbs all of the liquid (lard), let the skillet cook a little.
- Now add in all the saved squirrel-flavored water and a cup of thick cream.
- Put the pan back on the heat and allow the gravy to come to a slow boil.
- Keep stirring the gravy so that it does not stick.
- After a few minutes of boiling, taste for salt and pepper.
- Let the gravy simmer until it starts to thicken. Please keep in mind that only after the gravy gets cool does it thicken all the way.

How thick should good squirrel gravy be? Well, it should set on top of the biscuit so you don't have to go chasing it around the plate. Please remember that squirrel gravy should be free of all lumps. Now lumps don't necessarily hurt the taste of squirrel gravy or any gravy, for that matter. You just don't want others to know you ate lumpy gravy.

Serving Suggestions:

You will need some fresh cat-headed biscuits, some yellow cow butter, cold sweet milk, and honey. Now, take about three biscuits and pull them apart. I always ate six; three might be enough for a person your size.

Put a large piece of butter in the middle of each biscuit. I like to turn mine upside down so that the butter can soak into the top. In just a few seconds open up one and pour on some honey. You can go on and eat this one if you want to. The honey biscuit is just there to get your palate clean and sharpened for the squirrel gravy.

Very carefully turn the biscuits right side up and put the others of them in the center of your plate and open them up. Spoon on as much gravy as the biscuits can hold. Try not to let it run off of the sides. But, if it does, that is ok. I like to sprinkle on some more pepper -- not a lot, just enough to see it.

Get the fried squirrel out of the warming oven. I pour a large glass of sweet milk and enjoy. You truly do not need anything more than honey, fried squirrel and gravy, butter and cat-headed biscuits.

Now, some do like strong back coffee with this meal. It is just according to their taste.

The Good Times, the Bad Times, Pepper Steak and Fancy Rice

It is funny, I think, that when I was growing up all the times were good times. Now, as I look back, not everything was so good. There were a few hungry times, when there just wasn't much and that is the pure truth. Fortunately, bad times were few and far between.

I think what I am trying to say here can be summed up in one statement made by Aunt Toot. Toot said she had a real good ham bone she had been using for a good while to cook brown beans. She loaned it to a neighbor who cooked cabbage with it and ruined it.

You could tell exactly where we were in the payday cycle, and how much money could be spent on food. When times were good, Mom made fried salmon cakes. Well, they were not real salmon cakes; they were mackerel cakes. Daddy said, "The truth is only people in town eat salmon anyway. People out in the country eat mackerel cakes. They have a lot more real fish flavor."

As slow-headed as I was, I knew mackerel was cheaper. I just loved the cakes; I did not give one whit whether they were salmon or mackerel. Good times were here right now, and we hoped they would last forever.

When times were on the downhill side Mom would go to the garden and pick tomatoes, onions, some corn that was just a little past roasting ears, and lots of peppers. She liked the green and red ones; me, too. On the way back to the house she would stop by the chicken house and look down into the freezer. If she could reach one of the last small packages of hamburger, she brought it to the house to make us pepper steak.

If she could not reach the hamburger she made Fancy Rice. Often she made Fancy Rice because there was no hamburger. When we sat down to eat Mom and Daddy just looked across the table at one another. Nothing needed to be said. The $3.00 spent on a bottle of bootleg liquor could have been spent on a pack of hamburger. No complaint, now. I am as fat as a town dog.

Another key indicator of the paycheck running out before the week did was potato salad. Mom would make a boiled potato salad with an egg, mustard and mayonnaise dressing. There was little else to eat and this spread out the egg so everyone got some of it. I did like the potato salad.

Today, I almost never eat rice. I have not eaten pepper steak in years. I won't even eat potato salad at the family reunion. I do not think it's because it brings up bad memories. I ate so much of the stuff that I just don't want it. I can do a little better on my personal menu. Hell, let the past live in your memory. I have a feeling the past is done and over with, and I don't want to go looking for it either.

Here is what you need:

- Five or six cups of dry rice
- One cup of whole milk
- Ten good solid peppers – green, red and yellow if they are in the garden
- Ten dead-ripe tomatoes – red and yellow ones
- Ten good onions
- One or two ears of corn
- Two tablespoons of lard, if it is still good. If it isn't, use Crisco.
- Hamburger
- A piece of waxed paper
- 1/2 teaspoon of salt and 3/4 teaspoon of black pepper

Now, here is what you do:

- Put yesterday's rice in a large cast iron skillet to warm up. Or, boil your fresh rice if you're starting from scratch.
- Add the milk to the rice and cook until the milk is bubbly hot.
- Peel all the onions and cut the corn off of the cob.
- Peel the tomatoes and chop them up and put them in a bowl.
- The second the rice is hot or cooked, dump in the tomatoes, pepper, corn and onions and mix it all up. Add in the salt and pepper. Let it cook on low heat until almost all the liquid has evaporated out. This can be done on the top of the stove.
- Peel off a piece of waxed paper, put it on the counter, put the hamburger on top and start mashing it out as thin as you can.
- When the rice and vegetables are cooked, using the waxed paper as a holder, flip the thin hamburger onto the top of the mixture to cook.
- To serve try to cut it like a pie so that everyone gets a piece of hamburger.
- To make fancy rice, just add lots more rice and no hamburger.

A Real Man's Duck Hunt and Other Stuff

When I was a boy, my friends and I were meat hunters; I had heard of sportsmen, but I had not seen one of them yet. Duck hunting on the coldest days of the year was our favorite. I must have liked the hunting part better that than the killing part, because I never could hit a bull in the butt with a handful of beans. I still cannot. For the most part, ducks always felt safe when they looked down and saw me.

About 1971 or thereabout, a friend and I were working on a local farm. That spring we had planted corn on every hillside and river bottom. Truly there was corn everywhere. At the south end of one cornfield was a good-sized pond surrounded by big white oaks. Each fall in early October and November, large numbers of wood duck would come to that pond. Wood ducks are the first ducks to migrate south. Often they come and depart long before duck season starts.

By the pond in the spring, these same ducks, with family-raising on their minds, would use nesting boxes in the white oaks. In the fall they'd just eat corn for a day or two and rest up a little before flying off in search of a better wintering home. But, one October morning I was shelling corn in an adjoining field when I saw lots of wood ducks flying overhead -- one group after another headed for the pond.

About then, my brother showed up. I took the plug out of my trusty Remington 870 Wing Master and loaded it with five shells. I had five more in my mouth ready to reload. My brother had his old double barrel. We got down on our bellies and crawled up the pond dam, then stood up and started shooting. The ducks were so confused that they just made a circle around the pond. The whole hunt could not have lasted more than 90 seconds. But, in the end we took 26 wood ducks home for picking.

You see, duck season was still a good month away. I think the limit for wood ducks was most likely two per day. And no, we did not have hunting licenses. We grew up just like the men living on the River Ridge, who would have done the exact same thing and never thought twice about it. Now, I did not say it was right; I am just saying we were following a family code here. I can bet that if Mr. Johnny Morris, the local game warden, had come calling he would have taken both guns and my old truck, plus given us a major fine. That said, we were meat hunters anyway and were not into the sport of hunting. But, supper would be a good one!

Here is what you need:

- Make sure the duck is picked and singed off real close.
- A big wood duck may not weigh much more than two or three pounds at the most when cleaned, so be aware that it will cook real quick. They can be right fat, too.
- Salt, pepper and poultry seasoning
- 1/2 teaspoon of garlic powder
- A cup each of chopped celery, onions, apples
- About 4 tablespoons of honey and peach jelly

Now, here is what you do:

- A duck is a very fat bird. Unless you like the taste of fat, it is good idea to boil it for a few minutes just to get some of the fat out. So parboil rapidly for four or five minutes, or less. You be the judge of how much fat there is.
- Cut the oven on to 450 degrees, just to get it real hot.
- Dry off the duck and rub it with lots of butter and the garlic powder.
- Put the duck on a roasting pan resting on an elevated rack.
- Fill the cavity with celery, onions, and apples.
- Add salt, pepper and poultry seasoning to taste.
- Put the duck into the hot oven and cut the heat down to 350 degrees
- Cook covered about 20 minutes per pound or until tender. (Keep thinking that the duck cooked some while you were parboiling it.)
- When it is about 15 minutes from done, remove the top and paint the duck with honey and peach jelly.

Serving suggestions:

Serve this duck with fresh fall turnip greens, onions, cornbread, fried potatoes and apple dumplings, if you've got them. Some people are known to eat pinto beans with their duck. Beans are great too, but you've got to be careful. With beans, you will want a dish of right sweet coleslaw or slow-cooked parsnips or boiled turnips.

Mom says this recipe will not work with a goose, because they are far too greasy and the fat has to boil out some first.

Fried Mountain Oysters

One of the funniest practical jokes I ever played was done purely by accident. A mountain oyster is just pure meat with a bad name. Most know what a mountain oyster is, but for those who don't, it is a bull's, or buck sheep's or boar hog's testicles. I guess being the male reproductive organ has given them a bad name or something. Anyway some folks like them; some don't. As for me I can take them or leave them. When I was about 15 years old I was called to a friend's house to help castrate a big boar hog. I was big for my age, so I was called to help with jobs no other person on this earth would do. Some said that I was strong, too. I was just what they were looking for—big, strong and not too smart. Yes, that was me in a nutshell.

I truly think my services were an excuse for the boys—that being really the men in our family and their friends—to happen by looking for bootleg liquor, since this particular friend (the one with the boar hog) was a bootlegger, too. Anyway, he told me to take a piece of lumber, and hold that boar hog next to the fence and the rest of them will grab him. He was going to castrate him. Holding a 150-pound hog is harder than it looks.

Well, I did it, and he did his job. I knew when it was over. I heard him say, "I'll eat you son while you keep on growing."

Moving forward, I am about 18 or 20 years old I think. It is the first day of trout season. In Appalachia, all work is supposed to stop on Christmas, Easter and the first day of trout season. I had gotten a call on the Friday before start of trout season from a man who had bought a truckload of 500-pound bulls, and they needed to be castrated. He wanted to know if I could help the local veterinarian the next morning. Yes, but I needed to be finished and at the creek by 11:00 o'clock. (Trout season always started at noon.) We began just as soon as the sun was up good and finished by 10:00 a.m., having collected up a five-gallon bucket half full of mountain oysters.

At our fishing buddy's log cabin there was an electric stove on the outside. As long as you were standing on a brick pallet you could cook without being shocked too badly. Two of us sat down on an old log on the edge of the creek to shuck the oysters. We put them in a little still pool in the edge of the creek until it was time to cook them. After a while we baked up some of them canned biscuits and set them oysters to frying. All you had to do was wipe them dry and dip them in white flour and put them in a frying pan. When they are kind of crispy around the edges they are ready.

Before this day I had never eaten a mountain oyster, nor had I wanted to either. In the beginning, all I wanted to do was taste them. I found them to be quite tasty. They were a little mushy, but good. So you had to add some mustard to them.

Now, they smelled very good cooking. Fishermen walking by would ask for one. If you did not know about the stove's mean nature, you could get hurt. We'd tell them to help themselves, because if they did not know about that stove, simply put, they would get the mortal hell, knocked out of them. It was not grounded. It was a shocking experience, and it was funny to watch. Two of the men came by and made themselves a biscuit. After that they saw the leftover pieces in the creek as they fished on downstream. They whooped and hollered with laughter. If they had seen the leftover first, they would not have eaten the biscuit. But, they were now old-time oysters-eaters so they came back for more. Watching them was a good show. People came by wanting nut biscuits until they ran out.

Billy Joe Henry's reaction was the best of all. Billy Joe made hisself two biscuits, put a little mustard on them, and started eating. "Why are you boys giving away tenderloin biscuits? Did you all just kill hogs or something?"

I did not know what to say; so I said nothing. Billy Joe fished on down the creek a little ways and came up on the leftover parts, and he got real mad. He took to cussing. When he came back I just said "yessir" a lot until he cooled off.

As for me, the mountain oysters were okay; I do not want a steady diet of them. But for Billy Joe, he acted like we had force-fed him some new kind of poison. From then until now, I look each and every free biscuit right in the eye.

Here is what you do:

- It is best to collect your own, so you know just how fresh they are.
- Shuck off the outer skin and let them soak for a while.
- Clean and wash them off; then dry on a paper towel.
- Roll them in a buttermilk and egg mixture, then in a bowl of flour to cover both sides.
- Very gently lay them in a cast-iron skillet with hot lard. I do hope that you do not have to use Crisco, but it will do if you don't have any lard.
- Quickly slide the oysters around in the lard to keep them from sticking.
- Add salt and cover them black with pepper.
- Turn them over only one time.
- When mountain oysters are golden brown on both sides, they are done.
- Take them out of the grease and lay them on a paper towel.

Serving suggestions:

Hot biscuits, mayonnaise, mustard, fresh leaf lettuce and slices of tomato. I think that thin slices of onion would be good, too.

In West Tennessee, mountain oysters were served with collard greens, purple-hull peas, and chili pepper cornbread and egg slices.

No pinto beans are needed unless you just want them.

Boiled Ham and the Pickle I Like to Remember

It was either just before Thanksgiving or just before Christmas, I cannot remember which. I was about 8 years old. Dad and I had gone to the smokehouse to get two salt-cured hams that we carried to a table in the backyard. He built a big fire under a 15- or 20-gallon black cast-iron pot, while I carried water from Grandmother's house. As the water heated to a low boil, we cleaned off most of the salt and trimmed off dark-colored meat and some fat.

The hams were looking so good. Once they were cleaned and washed, and the water was boiling, we put each one in its own white cloth bag that looked something on the order of a pillowcase.

I sat by the pot most of the day as they slowly boiled. I just added a little wood to the fire and kept the water level just right. I bet you could smell them all the way back to the railroad gate. I could not wait to sink my teeth into a boiled ham biscuit. When the ham was cooked, we took it to the house.

To my surprise, this time one of the hams went to the car. Dad and I then drove up the road to another house. He made me go. I did not like the idea of giving away a good ham. At this house, they were truly poor. It was a place without a father or anyone who worked. I carried a ham and groceries into the house, while Dad talked. I just set the food on the kitchen table and we left. The only thing Dad said was, "Poor people need to eat, too, and you aren't ever to talk about this kind of thing ever again. Just know that when we eat tonight so will they."

It did not take me very long to understand why Dad did what he did. They needed help and for a few days, they ate just like me. They had not carried any water or mixed up chop or pulled bull weeds or hoed one hill of corn for the hogs like I had. Today, I am glad Dad made me go with him. Some of life's lessons are hard, but real quick and simple. I started the day poor and ended the day much better off.

I never heard another word about this. I am now 57 years old and not long ago I told this story to a woman who remembered how often "the boys" told her how much they appreciated the ham and the bag of groceries. I guess I had forgotten, but they have not.

Yes, my dad and his brothers were rough customers, but they had a good side too. They were exceptional people brought up in exceptional times

How to cure a country ham:

- As soon as the body heat is out of the meat you can start to trim it into shape.
- Save all scrap meat and fat for sausage.
- In a bowl combine 1/2 pound of salt, one pound of white sugar, two tablespoons of black pepper and a tablespoon of saltpeter.
- Rub this mixture all over the ham.
- Either put the ham in a white cotton sack and hang it up in the smokehouse for a year or lay the ham on the meat table in the smokehouse. We mostly laid the hams in the smokehouse.
- In about three weeks we took them out of the smokehouse and washed off the salt. Then we rubbed a much thinner layer of salt and sugar into the meat. (Some people like to use brown sugar rather than white.)
- In about eight weeks the ham is fully cured.

Just How Do You Boil a Ham Anyway:

- First, you go get the old black cast-iron pot out of the smokehouse and drag it to the cooking spot.
- Scrub the iron pot with lots of soap and water to get off all of the old lard that was rubbed on last fall to it to keep it from rusting.
- Set a large orange flint rock under each of the pot's legs.
- Fill the pot about half full of cold water, before you start the fire.
- Start a very small fire under the pot, one no bigger than the rocks the pot is setting on. You do not want to crack the cast-iron pot; it has to be warmed up real slow. This is truly important enough to say two times: warm that pot up very slowly.
- Go to the smokehouse and take a ham out and wash off the salt and trim off anything that you don't like.
- Put the ham in a clean white cloth bag about the size of a pillowcase. Now put it in the warming water.
- Bring the water to a low boil and cook for about five hours; then hang the cloth bag up on the clothesline to drain for a little while.
- Put the ham on a big flat pan and slice it as thin as possible.

Serving suggestions:

Boiled country ham is a true River Ridge delicacy! A meal like this needs to planned and not rushed into. Timing here is everything, and there is more preparation than with a regular meal.

After the ham is cooling, collect up at least one gallon of the juices from the cast-iron pot. While you are out, go to the garden and pull out a head of cabbage that was buried last fall. Go to the cellar and get some potatoes, turnips and a few parsnips. About five or six onions are needed, too. Get a jar of canned cherries and two jars of green beans. With the ham juice, make milk gravy.

Make a fresh pan of biscuits or hot rolls and set out the butter and honey.

Fry the potatoes, onions, turnips and parsnips together in one pan with some lard and some of the ham juice. Cook the green beans with salt-cured bacon on top. If there are any kale and turnip greens left in the garden, now is the time to cook them.

Bake a big cherry cobbler and whip thick cream for a topping.

The key here is this meal has all got to come to the table at about the same time! There is art to this kind of cooking, and my mother and grandmother knew exactly how to do it. You can even set out the good dishes if you want to.

Elmer would say, "A meal like this will make your belly toot out like morning glory."

Beef Stew: The More Modern River Ridge Style

Beef stew is one of the mainstays of every Appalachian American. When I was a child, early in the morning, Mother would put a big chuck roast in a large stew pot, and it would set on the stove to boil. She put in a lot of onions, potatoes, and carrots, plus some salt and some black pepper; she added a gallon of water. I mean she let it boil. She set it on the old wood stove and forget about it. It would cook from about breakfast until it was time to serve. I did like it. The meat would have cooked tender and the vegetables were gone somewhere. I think that they were now part of the juices in the bottom of the stew pot. Now it was good; lots of fat little boys grew up eating stew made this way.

Over the past 50 years, I have made a few changes in the way I make this family favorite. I now use a crock-pot and no water. Please give this new method a try. It has more flavors and just as much rib-sticking capacity. I find this to be a great stimulus for snow shoveling. And I use this dish to entertain guests.

Here is what you need:

- Six pounds of arm roast. Do not cut the meat into cubes.
- Two pounds of mushrooms – the smaller ones are best, but any will do.
- Two large onions, two large potatoes, three carrots and three stalks of celery. Just hold onto them; we will chop them later.
- Two tablespoons of salt and of garlic
- One tablespoon each of pepper, cayenne pepper, marjoram, thyme, cumin, bay leaves (the crumbled kind)
- 1/2 tablespoon of rosemary and ginger
- I like to go on and measure out the spices and put them in a little bowl. Give them a quick shake.
- One cup of whole milk – only if you need a few juices

Now, here is what you do:

- After breakfast, put the roast in the crock-pot and sprinkle in one half of the spices. Turn the roast over and sprinkle the other half of the spices. Turn the crock-pot on high, and let the chuck roast cook for six or seven hours.
- Take the meat out of the pot and put it in a sturdy glass dish and place it in the refrigerator overnight. Collect all the liquid; there should not be much. Let the liquid cool overnight.
- About eight hours before serving, remove almost all of the fat from the liquids. With a potato masher mash up the meat some and stir it around a little to separate the meat fibers. Put the meat and juices back in the clean crock-pot and turn it to high.
- About four hours before serving stir in the milk. Let milk come to room temperature before pouring it into the crock-pot. Take a small dish out and taste and adjust your seasonings. Turn the crock-pot to low.
- Cut the potatoes, carrots, celery and onion into uniform 1/2-inch pieces. About 90 minutes before serving, add the vegetables and stir once or twice.
- About 30 minutes before serving adjust spices and add in the two pounds of mushrooms.

Serving suggestions:

I like to have the meat cooked until each strand of meat is separated. Plus, I like the vegetables to be cooked at the moment I serve the beef stew. If all goes well, there will be very few juices at all.

I serve the beef stew with cornbread and a tossed salad.

As for wine, I like to pour a Syrah. I personally think that it has a certain spicy quality that pairs well with the stew. But the last time I made this dish a neighbor brought a Spanish Tempranillo. Both were very good.

FISH
OR
FAMINE

Gigging

When I was a kid growing up, going gigging was about the best thing there ever was. Gigging fish was something that almost all men in the area did. I think growing up during the Depression, as they had, made you search for ways to find a little extra free food and simple entertainment.

Some of the lure of gigging was getting together with friends to eat a little, fish some and drink some liquor. Oh, and catch a fish or two. Maybe they relived doing just what their daddies had done. Today they call this kind of stuff male bonding.

The boat-poler had the most important job. He moved the boat across the river as the gigger held the car light and slowly and methodically searched the clear river water for fish. The boat-poler needed to see the fish at the same time as the gigger. The poler then slowly and quietly moved the boat toward the unsuspecting fish.

While the fish was being blinded by the car light, the gigger soused the gig into his back and pressed him to the bottom. Only when the fish was sufficiently attached to the gig was it lifted from the bottom and thrown into the boat. Often when the gig was removed the fish got real mad and went to flopping and slinging mud and blood everywhere. Sometimes there was a third person in the boat; he was the sacker.

Mom always gave out orders that I was not to be left alone. See, Mom thought it would be a good idea for my safety and all. Daddy and his friends misunderstood the true meaning of the instruction. They heard Mom say, "Charles can hunt for firewood all night long, skin fish and put cleaned fish in a tub, keep all the water, mud, blood and muck dipped out of the boat." I was also responsible for keeping up with all the beer. It was usually sitting in the edge of the river with rocks holding it down. Often there were three or four bottles of liquor there too. A quart jar of clear moonshine was never far away.

Men came to visit and possibly to keep in touch with their own youth and, of course, to hear the retelling of the old stories. I kept the fire going, and the men kept the storytelling going. When the fire was just right, I was told to look around in the weeds and find the skillet and coffee pot. I would carry them to the river's edge and scrub them with sand until they were as shiny as a new penny. Someone would have gone to the weeds and pulled out that old metal sliding board we used as a cook top to set pots and pans on. By now, the men would have pulled out fresh sausage or pork chops and the feasting part would start.

Gigging in the spring meant eating canned beef and sausage from the cellar or meat from the freezer. Summer gigging meant meat eating and all kinds of fresh vegetables right out of the garden, along with early harvest apples and the last of the canned sausage.

Plus there were tomatoes fried in the sausage grease. The recipe was simple. Roll the green tomatoes in flour and egg and drop them into about an inch and a half of sausage grease. They were so good that I hear about their virtue every time I go to the doctor. I can still see the results each time I step on the scales or try to find my feet. Why, once I got on the scales and the little hand went around two times and flew off; cracked the little window too. But, still I like fried green tomatoes. They taste good. All of the foods and experiences produced wonderful memories.

I remember corn roasted in the shucks. There were always little patches of field corn planted along the river. It was ten feet tall and much tougher than sweet corn. But, it was great when it was freshly picked, slow roasted in the gigging fire and coupled with the smell of sausage and tomatoes. Peel back the blackened shucks, sprinkle with salt and add a little yellow cow butter. It really was great. Uncle Shorty told me once: "The people in town are the ones that eat sweet corn, because their teeth are right tender. You keep eating this field corn and your teeth will be strong and tough."

Another gigging food that cannot be omitted is the little red potatoes and onions fried in salt-cured bacon grease. Sometimes we would take some of the fish that I had just cleaned and drop large pieces into the boiling grease. That too was good. I like fried catfish best with fried bread or fried biscuit dough.

There finally came a time when I graduated from my bank duties. Well, somehow I graduated into the third person in the boat. I had to get all of the potatoes and onions dug, and the tenderest of the corn pulled and carried to the fire site. I stacked a small mountain of firewood next to the food and gathered a bucket of tomatoes. Later in the summer I always needed five or six "musk melons." For you town people, that is a cantaloupe.

I needed to find up the coffee pot and the skillet and scrub them clean as a pen. It was a wonder that we did not die from food poisoning. As I got a little older Mom would send along a few rags and dish detergent. Nothing could kill that bunch of old drunk men, but she figured they just might not be as tough as you think. You see, the frying pan was always left full of grease so that it would not rust too much. I guess river water and sand cleaned all of the old grease and animal tracks and food poisoning out of it.

Salt Fish

My daddy and his brothers put up some homemade salt fish. By my time making a barrel of salt fish had passed on to become something only the old timers did or even talked about. We made only a few gallons of salt fish, because the men just wanted the kids to see how it was done.

But, in those days every little country store had at least one barrel of salt fish for sale. No matter where you got them, you truly had to be a tough person to eat salt fish. You needed to be a real man to get them out of the barrel. You took a big fork, opened up the barrel and dug through the salt, funky water, fish scales and who knows what else. I can tell you that when the lid was off of the barrel even the air in the store took on a strong, bad taste. In fact, it was so strong that the store cats ran to the front door for a breath of fresh air.

You took the fish home and set them to soaking, changing the water once or twice a day for two days or more, then carefully cut the bones out. When you were satisfied all of the salt was out and most of the bones, you dipped the fish in an egg batter, rolled them in flour and cornmeal and fried them right crispy. Mom would also fry them with eggplant for breakfast.

About everyone ate salt fish, but some folks were better than others at leaching out the salt. Keep in mind: if you soaked them for a week you could not get all the salt out.

When you got to school you could tell whose parents spent the most time getting the salt out. For example, if you stopped by the water fountain and drank hard and steady for, say, two to four minutes, your parents had worked real hard on leaching out the salt. But, if the kid in front of you laid his or her arm up on the water fountain and settled in for a while, it was a sure sign those parents had rushed the soaking process. Either that or the youngster has done caught the hydrophobia. In a real soft and sympathetic voice, the teacher would say: "Just go on to the room and set down. Hang in there. You can get you some water after awhile."

Today, I see salt herring in small jars in a meat case at the grocery store, but I don't even slow down to look. Some parts of the past are just painful.

Here is what you need:

- Eight or ten salt herrings just picked out of the barrel
- Wash the salt fish in clear, clean water at least three times. Let them soak overnight at least one time to get some of the salt out.
- Cut out the bones, if you wish.
- Two cups of corn meal
- One cup flour
- Two cups of fresh lard
- Pepper (NO SALT NEEDED)
- Three eggs and a cup of milk
- Popcorn for testing

Now, here is what you do:

- Set the cast-iron skillet on the stove with a cup of lard. Let the lard get hot.
- Take the fish out of the water and pat them dry with a towel.
- In a large bowl dump the flour and cornmeal. Add in some pepper, but not too much. You know about how much you like.
- In a right large bowl crack the eggs and pour in the milk and stir them up with a fork.
- Use the popcorn to test the heat – when the popcorn pops, eat the kernels and put the salt fish in the hot lard.
- Roll the fish in the egg and milk bowl.
- Quickly roll the fish in flour and cornmeal.
- Slowly place the fish in the lard and move it around a little so it doesn't stick.
- Do this over and over until the cast-iron skillet is full.
- When the first fish is brown on the bottom, it is time to turn them beauties over.
- Cook them fish until they are right crispy-looking.

Serving suggestions:

For breakfast, I would suggest two or three fried eggs, a few hot cat-headed biscuits, lots of yellow cow butter, fried apples, blackberry or raspberry jelly, strong black coffee and sweet milk. Up in the winter, a big glass of cold tomato juice would be nice, too.

For lunch, I would suggest having cold biscuits cut in half and toasted with lots of yellow mustard. Again, cold milk is nice. Really good is a big dish of coleslaw made from a head of cabbage dug from the buried pile of vegetables in the edge of the garden. A pan of hot sauerkraut would be good, too. If you have them, a dish of fried turnips would fit in very well. I also like sweet apple pie with salt fish. Drink a big glass of water before you go back outside, cause you are going to need it!

For supper, I would suggest a dish of sauerkraut from the barrel in the cellar. I like to have cornbread with lots of butter. Pinto beans cooked all day on the back of the woodstove, cooked down until they are so thick that chunks of onion just set right up on top and don't even try to sink. Two or three tablespoons of chowchow right on top of the beans. A big glass of buttermilk covered with black pepper is great with this dish. If there is any buttermilk left, now would be a great time to use it up.

Be forewarned. If you eat salt fish for all three meals you most likely will drink the spring dry. I encourage you to use moderation.

Fried Catfish and Other Kinds of Fish, Too

When I say fish, I am meaning to say catfish. Catfish is the quintessential river fish. My, my, the flesh is light in color. The meat is real flakey and the taste is out of this world. It is no wonder that so many men set trotlines when I was a kid.

A little note here: As a child I thought that people all over the whole world ate catfish. Later I learned that catfish was considered a trash fish by some, because they are bottom-feeders. Another most interesting point is that within the catfish eating population there are different sects. One group only likes mud cats. While another group of people choose to eat only blue cats or channel cats. As, for me I harbor no bad feelings against any catfish. For me, there are only three kinds: great, extremely good and magnificent.

Now, this recipe can be put to use on red-eyes, bass, bluegills, you name it. You can get real fancy if you wish. I have added lemon juice, lemon zest, hazelnut crumbs in the flour. But you are going to find that this simple recipe will get the job done.

Here is what you need:

- Skin or scale your fish. You need at least one pound for fillets. You can cook the whole fish, too. I will leave that up to you.
- A cup of lard or Crisco
- Salt and pepper
- Cayenne pepper
- A bowl with about two cups of cornmeal

Now, here is what you do:

- Get your cast-iron skillet hot with about 1/2 inch of lard. (If you like, test the heat with popcorn.)
- Add in salt and pepper to the cornmeal and mix.
- Dip all the pieces of fish in the cornmeal and set them on a clean plate for a minute so the meal will stick good.
- Once the popcorn pops the lard is real hot.
- Take one fish piece at a time and slowly place it in the pan. Move it around a little before you turn it loose. This will help to keep the fish from sticking.
- If you like, you can add a little cayenne pepper to the raw side of the fish, but you don't have to.
- Fish cook fast, so be ready to turn them over as soon as the pan side is brown. Don't overcook!

Serving Suggestions:

Well, a big dish of sauerkraut is almost a must. Hot cornbread is a true must. Lots of yellow cow butter is needed, too. I like a big plate of fresh canned greens. Brown beans and chowchow are awful good with fried fish. Now, here is ringer for you. They are awfully good with fried eggplant. Lots of sweet milk is important. If sweet potatoes can be had, they are good too. Elmer always liked buttermilk with fried fish, and everyone likes berry cobblers.

Sometimes Mama would mix the leftover green beans and brown beans. They were awful good. Mama liked to add lots of onions, black pepper and a big shake of vinegar. The vinegar was good with salt fish.

Fried Fish Roe

Mother was from Richmond, Virginia, and they ate different foods down there. Things like fried eggplant, stuffed veal, and fish roe.

Now, that last one is something that we did eat. Like I often say, if it ran slow or did not have too many stickers on it, we ate it.

Mom loved fish roe. Fish roe are the little sack of eggs in the fish. You find them when you gut the fish. We collected them from bass, catfish, red-eyes and perch. I would save every little sack for Mom.

Here is what you need:

- About one pound of fresh fish roe from river fish
- Salt
- Lard
- Some popcorn
- Flour
- One or two eggs

Now, here is what you do:

- Wash fish roe in salt water and do not break the little egg sacks.
- Heat up a pan with about 1/2 inch of lard. The lard needs to be deep enough to cook both the top and bottom at the same time.
- Test the temperature with popcorn.
- Roll the roe in a bowl of eggs and then in a bowl of flour.
- Here is the tricky part: pick up the fish roe with a spoon and gently lay it in the hot grease and kind of swish it around for one or two seconds. This way it won't stick. Please make sure the grease is hot when you drop the fish roe in or they will get real greasy and it will be real hard to chew them. Also, they stick easily and then you have got a real big mess.

Serving Suggestions:

Mom always ate fish roe for breakfast. I found it best served with lots of coffee, homemade biscuits with yellow cow butter and honey. The honey kind of cuts the grainy feel in my mouth.

Now, you had to keep both eyes on Momma Ruth; she is a tricky old bird. She was known to put fish roe in scrambled eggs. I did not like this because it made me think of Uncle Shorty and his "Hog Brains and Eggs."

Others thought it was a right tasty change.

HOW SWEET
IT IS

Grapes, Peaches, Cherries, Mulberries and Sour Apples

I think that the good Lord had redneck River Ridge Boys in mind when he made fresh fruit. In late spring it all got started in Mr. Otis Hampton's pasture. There were six cherry trees: two Black Hearts, two Sour and two just big sweet cherries. These trees were as large as the white oak in our backyard. About everyone in the area came and picked cherries to take home and make jelly, jam and pies. Me, I ate the fresh, unwashed fruit right off the tree. The family picked the cherries standing on the ground or on short ladders. That left all the fruit in top of the tree for me and the birds. I started down one limb, holding on with one hand picking and eating with the other. I ate until I could see cherries in my sleep.

Mostly, though, I remembered them in the toilet. I would eat so many that I could not pass a toilet. My bowels were in about the same shape as when Daddy passed our spring tonic. Once I got my stomach under control, I headed back to the cherry trees. When I started climbing, the birds would fly off. There would be so many that the sky would briefly darken. About

20 years ago Kevin Harris and me climbed the last remaining cherry tree and ate our fill. We did not look for worms or bad spots. We just ate the large black cherries until our stomachs ached. It is good sometimes to just remember.

Like last June, I stopped by the nursing home to visit Momma. She met me at the door with a big cup in her hand. For the past few weeks she had been watching the mulberries ripen on the tree near her window. We picked and ate mulberries until we were full. We carried a cup back into the nursing home. Aunt Kelly met us at the door. She, too, had been watching the tree. As she ate, she reminded me of how we picked and ate the mulberries from the big tree down in the holler. "We kept the bark wore thin," she said.

Back in the day, we even made mulberry pie, while Mr. Wilson made gallons of sweet mulberry wine.

After the cherry season passed, it wasn't long before the peaches started to show color. Just out Grandmother's back door was the best peaches in the whole world of River Ridge. There was a row of five clingstone peaches planted between the garden and the houses. Every morning I would race the chickens for the ones that had fallen during the night. I did not get to eat my fill of peaches, because Mamaw and my mother picked the tree so clean I was reduced to picking with the chickens.

One year there was an exceptionally large peach right in the top -- a big yellow with a kind of whitish stripe about it.

Grandmother told everyone to stop pitching rocks at it. Well, one day it was gone! I just about cried, until Shorty told me that he'd climbed up there and picked it for me so it would not get bruised from its fall to the ground. You can say what you like, but I think Uncle Shorty did like me. I ate the whole peach with Shorty and Grandmother refusing to take one bite. I think little things like that mean family!

Since I could not remember just exactly how Grandmother made peach dumplings, I had to ask my mother and she had to think about this for a day or two. Here is what we came up with. If it works, it is the right way. If they turn out to be real good, then I am just a one of those run-of-the-mill geniuses we hear about every once in while.

Here is what you need:

- About two cups of flour right out of the bag
- A tablespoon or so of salt
- 3/4 cup of yellow butter
- A little bit of water, not much. Peach juice can be used if any runs out of the fresh peaches.
- A little lemon juice to keep the peaches from turning brown
- Two or three tablespoons of white sugar
- No more than 3/4 teaspoon of cinnamon
- Six real big, fresh peaches, cut in half
- A cup of sugar
- About one cup of water
- One egg
- A cast-iron baking pan

Now, here is what you do:

- Mix the flour and salt.
- Pre-heat the oven to about 400 degrees.
- Pour the flour and salt into a bowl with the butter and mix it up with a fork and knife.
- Add an egg and a little water (or peach juice) and mix into flour until it looks like dough.
- Grease the cast-iron baking pan.
- Roll out the dough and sprinkle on the sugar and cinnamon.
- Cut the dough into small squares just big enough to cover the peach half.
- Put a small hunk of butter in each peach half and then put the peach half in the pan.
- Take 1/2 cup of sugar, boil it with a cup of water and pour this over the dish.
- Bake for a half an hour or until it is done.

Every house from Long Shop to Lovers' Leap had a Concord grapevine. Come August I checked out each and every one of them. I would just stand under the grape arbors and eat grapes by the bunch. It was hard to tell who got more -- mothers making jelly, birds or me.

One time I just happened to stumble across a pinkish-colored grape up near Prices Fork. I ate so many of them that I truly thought that my stomach would bust. No, I did not bust, but sure enough did break loose. After I got back to where I could walk, I went looking for more, but they had all been picked to make homemade wine. I learned that these were Catawba grapes. I never passed by that house that I didn't check on the development of the grapes. I never saw many Catawbas until I went to work for MJC Vineyards. Again, I ate them until I was sick, and I enjoyed every minute and each cramp.

In early fall I searched out every hard sour apple tree in the county. I'd pick them and sprinkle on a little salt. I ate them until frost. The main thing I remember about the fruit was the freedom to roam. I just went from house to house, yard to yard. No one ever hollered at me or said one negative thing. Once in a while, some of the grownups would join me. They would talk about the fine fruits they had eaten when they were kids. I thought it was funny that I was eating fruit from the same patches and trees that they had.

Today, I never see a young person going from yard to yard eating fresh fruit. Possibly scared of the worms? The homeowners? Or maybe it's just a lot easier to get fruit from the grocery store. I do not know exactly when it happened, but time has changed things on me and not always for the better, either.

Now, apple dumplings the way we ate them are a little different from peach dumplings. All you need is a few real hard apples, some butter, oatmeal, raisins and cinnamon.

Here is what you need:

- Eight hard Yellow Delicious or York or Smokehouse apples
- 1/2 pound of butter
- 1/4 teaspoon of cinnamon and about 1/4 teaspoon of salt
- 1/2 pound of raisins
- Three cups of oatmeal
- Two eggs
- Three tablespoons of brown sugar
- Just a very few fresh cracked black walnuts that you chop up into very little pieces.

Now, here is what you do:

- Core the apples.

- Grease the baking dish. I like cast-iron.

- In a bowl mix: butter, oatmeal, brown sugar, raisins, salt and cinnamon.

- Mix the eggs into the dry ingredients.

- Carefully fill each apple with the filling.

- Bake at 350 degrees until all of the fluid from apple and butter are soaked up.

- When the eggs are done the apple is ready to eat.

Pumpkin Pie
River Ridge Style

I do not know of anyone who doesn't like pumpkin pie. Me, I like to eat the pumpkin pie filling, too. Every fall we would fire up the old black cast-iron kettle in the backyard. One of the many things we cooked was pumpkins.

All of the bad pumpkins were fed to the hogs or cows. Each day one or two were chopped up with a corn cutter and pitched over the fence. The hogs came running. Hogs just love pumpkin.

The pumpkins not eaten by the animals, we ate. We would peel and then chop up 15 or 20 to fill two or three galvanized bathtubs. Once the fire was set under the cast-iron kettle, we'd pour in a coffee pot full of water so the pumpkin would not stick. After the water, Grandmother added in eight or ten of the very small pieces of pumpkin. I would start stirring just like making apple butter. Every so often more pumpkin was added until it all cooked into thick, pasty-looking goo. The thicker the goo, the better.

Once all the pumpkin was in the iron kettle and starting to cook down, Grandmother and Mom started lining up clean quart canning jars on the table on the screened-in porch. When the pumpkin was all but finished cooking, Grandmother (She was the head spicer.) added some salt, cinnamon, sugar and other spices. Everyone tasted it, and once we agreed that it tasted like pumpkin pie filling it was poured into the quart jars.

You could just open a jar and make pumpkin pie about anytime you wanted to. Spring, summer, winter and fall you could have a pumpkin pie. You could also add a cup or two of pumpkin to your morning pancake batter. Once in awhile Mom would open a jar and give me a dish of pumpkin to eat. I could eat the stuff anytime. It did not have to be made into a pie for me.

I guess I was about 15 years old when my friends and I were taking a break from picking up hay. We were setting on the porch of Long Shop Grocery eating lunch. I had my standard lunch: a big hunk of yellow cheese and two cans of Nancy Jo Kale. I washed all this down with a big double cola. Well, I was still a little hungry so I went back into the store, looked over the entire ready-to-eat foods section and spied a large can of pumpkin.

My thoughts went back to the dishes of pumpkin Mom once made and served me. When I came out of the store, in unison my friends and Mr. Rudisell, the store owner, said, "You cannot eat that stuff like that." Why the hell not? My mommy once made pumpkin pie filling for me. Before anyone could say another word I took a real big spoonful, gave it a big chew and spit the stuff out on the ground. Before this day I had never eaten straight pumpkin. I mean with no sugar, no cinnamon, no cloves, and no salt. It was right down bitter. Mr. Rudisell was right when he said I had run up on something that I could not eat. Today, my brother Melvin won't eat pumpkin. Something a cow would eat, he says.

Here is what you need:

- Cold lard
- A quart jar of pumpkin pie filling from the cellar
- A regular-size pie pan
- Regular flour
- Cold water
- Salt
- An egg

Now, here is what you do:

- Preheat the oven to 400 degrees.
- Mix two cups of regular flour and one teaspoon of salt. (DO NOT USE FLOUR WITH BAKING POWDER OR BAKING SODA ALREADY MIXED IN.)
- Take one cup of lard.
- Make a little hole in the middle of the flour and spoon in some lard and start cutting it with a knife and fork; add in some more lard and keep cutting it in. Sooner or later it will start getting a very coarse look about it. Keep cutting it until it is looks grainy. Add a spoon or two of water if it is needed.
- Now roll it up into a ball. Sprinkle flour on the dough board and roll it out to about 1/4 inch.
- Carefully pick up the dough and put it on the pie pan; fit the dough to the pan and cut off the rest. Take your fork and mash the edge all the way around the pie pan
- Pour the pumpkin pie filling into a large bowl. Taste and see if the spices are the way you like. Now add in the egg. Carefully spoon in the pie filling all the way to the top.
- Bake at 400 degrees until a toothpick comes out clean.

Pumpkin Persimmon Pie

Life is truly funny. A sound, a smell, a place or sometimes a word can trigger long-forgotten things and make those memories as real as just a few minutes ago. I had not thought anything about eating persimmons in a long time. A year or two ago I was standing in line at a local picture-framing establishment. There, beside the line, was a thick stack of posters. I started to thumb through the stack, and suddenly stopped when I came across a poster of four almost perfect persimmons. My mind went back to the persimmon trees in a field next to the house. I just stood there until the clerk started laughing at me.

As a kid I can remember climbing the two permission trees in the far end of the pasture near our house. I can see all of the River Ridge children standing under the persimmon trees daring each other to eat just one. No animal alive or dead would dare eat one of them before a very hard freeze. In the spring and summer they are green, and in the fall they take on a very nice, shiny, light-brownish-orange color. It is at this time every red-necked boy must give one of them a try, just to see if they are ripe. Before a freeze they are bitter and tannic as the green stuff in a hog's gallbladder. A green persimmon will turn your mouth wrong side out, and it will stay that way for an hour or longer.

But, you keep an eye on them! After a hard frost they start to get sweeter and after a hard freeze, just overnight permissions get as sweet as candy. It is at this point that if you are going eat any, you had better get at it. The opossums, squirrels, coons and foxes start to feast on permissions. A wild persimmon is nothing more than seeds and skin; there is very little fruit that a human can eat. So it takes lots.

Again I go to the nursing home to gain more information on cooking. I tell Mom that I could remember eating lots of raw permissions and once or twice eating cooked ones. How they were fixed I just could not remember. But, Mom did and the old ladies did, too. When I asked Mom, the flock of old ladies just came rolling over again to the table. Some had eaten them raw and occasionally one would mention that they had eaten them cooked.

I asked why we made these pies. "Well after Thanksgiving there were loads of pumpkins, and everyone had eaten about all they could stand. We did not need the persimmons for food, but we needed something a little different on the table."

Remember: do not eat too many persimmons at one time. They can make you knock the frost off the path to the outhouse!

Here is what you need:

- Three eggs
- 16 ounces of fresh boiled pumpkin – set the pumpkin in a colander to let some of the water drain out.
- One cup of persimmon fruit – you will need to pull off the skin and squeeze out the seeds. You need about 25 wild persimmons. They are right small. Make sure that there has been a hard freeze and wild animals are eating the ones on the ground.
- One quart of fresh-collected cream, both for the pie and for making whipped cream
- One cup of white sugar
- 1/2 cup of self-rising flour (Or, if you have a lot of cold rice in the refrigerator, you can put that in the place of the flour. Just make sure it is really dry.)
- 1/2 teaspoon of ground cloves
- 1/2 teaspoon of ground ginger
- 3/4 teaspoon of cinnamon
- 3/4 teaspoon of salt

Now here is what you do:

- Again, make sure the persimmons are dead ripe! I have seen people's tongues might near drop off from eating unripe persimmons. Ok, if you are satisfied, move on.
- In a large bowl put the eggs, fresh pumpkin, persimmons, 16 ounces of the cream, flour, spices. Mix everything up well.
- Either make a fresh pie crust or use a store-bought one.
- Empty the pie filling into the piecrust.
- Bake at 350 degrees for 45 minutes or until a broom-straw comes out clean.
- Take the remaining 16 ounces of fresh cream and whip until it is fluffy and white.
- You can serve your Pumpkin Persimmon Pie hot or cold.

Fried Apple Pies

The old road from Prices Fork through River Ridge came right behind my grandmother's house. I asked Mamaw once why in the world the road builders took such a meandering way when a straight line would have been much easier. Pasture grass and open ground that a farmer could work was at a premium. Country people did not have anywhere to go anyway, so why build much of road?

Now about all I can remember of the old place in the holler is the orchard. There were three pear trees and more than five kinds of apple trees. I like the two early harvest apple trees, one yellow and one kind of red. There is an early harvest yellow apple tree next to the old store in Prices Fork. Each summer when apples are ripe and falling, I stop and pick up one or two just to remember my youth. Down in the holler, I ate them until my stomach hurt. Man, they were sweet! About 15 years ago I found an apple seedling in the holler. I pulled it up and planted it at the family cemetery. It turned out to be the last of the early harvest red apples from the holler. Now I fight with worms, rabbits and deer to eat a few bites each year. They are still good and packed full of Grandmother's Stories!!

135

As a child I climbed the trees over by the cliff near the railroad in search of the best of the best apples. I learned early that the best ones are right in the top, where the sun and wind have had their way with them. I think my favorite apple was from a tree that one of my uncles was said to have planted. Mamaw said her brother had eaten this apple somewhere on one of his many short travels and brought home the seeds in his pocket. Everyone called it a "Rambo" or "Smokehouse" apple. In the fall it was as hard as a rock, but by New Year's it was soft and mellow. It was known all over the world and River Ridge as a fried pie apple. From a seed to apple-bearing may take 15 to 20 years. By my time these were giant trees. Today even their stumps have long since rotted away. But, I still know where they were and how the fruit tasted.

In the early fall I would pick up sacks full of apples and use the horse sled to carry them to the house. Not long ago I stood in front of one of the fraternity houses on the Virginia Tech campus and ate fallen apples for an hour. Every student walking by just looked at me. Not one had a clue of my memories of doing this 50 years ago, down in the holler below Grandmother's. As she fried up apple pies, Mamaw told me about the old people that once lived along the road and down in the holler.

We had apples so we ate them. All of the apples on the ground were picked up and taken to the hog lot. Pigs liked apples too. I only ate the picked off the tree kind.

Here is what you need:

- At least three gallons of early transparent apples peeled and cut into slices
- The big cast-iron skillet
- SEE THE PIE DOUGH RECIPE MENTIONED EARLIER, in the Pumpkin Pie Recipe
- Lard
- Salt
- Sugar and cinnamon

Now, here is what you do:

- Put about 1/2 cup of lard in the big cast-iron skillet.
- When it gets hot, add in the apples and cook them down until they are almost applesauce.
- Make up the fresh pie dough or get it out of the refrigerator to warm up.
- Sift some flour on the dough board and roll out the dough until it is a little less than 1/4 inch thick. Cut circles about six inches in diameter
- Add spices to taste: While the apples are cooking add in salt, sugar and cinnamon. (Sometimes Grandmother would use brown sugar instead of white sugar.)
- Now, here is an important step! Once the apples are the way you like, pour them into a bowl and set them close to the pie dough. Carefully wipe out the big cast-iron pan, add in about 1/2 cup of lard, and let it melt and get hot. Test the temperature with popcorn. If you put the pie in the lard too quickly, it will be greasy.
- Spoon apples into the pie dough, fold it over and crimp the edges with a fork.
- Make up five or six apple pies
- Real careful-like lay them in the hot lard one at a time and move each around a little so it doesn't stick.
- Cook the pies for two or three minutes on each side.
- Set them on a plate to cool.

Serving suggestions:

Now, fried apple pies must be served correctly or they are not as good. Put one on a little saucer and dust it with powdered sugar.

You need a big glass of cold, sweet milk to drink along with the pie.

Fried pies, fried eggs, fried salt bacon and fresh strong coffee are recommended if you are eating your pies for breakfast. You can also carry them wrapped in wax paper to school, and every kid will want to trade you their lunch for your pie.

The Old Standard Apple Pie

One thing I liked about the apples trees was the fact they kept me camouflaged from the world, at least I thought so. I would climb up into the little limbs no bigger around than a cigarette, just set and wave in the wind like a bird. I would imagine I was in the airplanes going over. Speaking of cigarettes, I would practice my cigarette smoking, too.

Somehow I did not take into account the fact that the top of the apple tree was just about level with Grandmother's porch. She could sit in her rocker and look right at me. For some reason I never looked back at her. I guess I was about eight years old when one day I came down and Mother and Grandmother were waiting for me. They were very mad and all worked up over something.

"Where did you get those cigarettes?" Well, I took to crawfishing and double-talking and walking backward. They nailed me. "You stole them cigarettes from Uncle Shorty, didn't you?"

I just had to come clean, "Yes I did." Well, they did give my butt a working over, you know what I mean? They made it feel like it had been stuck right on a barbecue grill. I got over it quickly. They never questioned my smoking cigarettes; they just wanted me not to steal any more. I love apple trees.

After Mom had beat the hell out of me she would show up with a plate of apple slices. If they were the hard, sour ones she would have sprinkled them with salt. If they were the sweet ones, she would have sprinkled them with cinnamon. Today, I still eat apples the same way.

Mr. Jack Morris lived up the road from us a few miles. He was eating pie one time and said that in places around the world people put cheese on apple pie. Sounded good, but we never tried it. Apple pie was ok the way it was. That was the same day that Mr. Morris informed us that he'd been visiting his children in another state where they don't peel cucumbers; they eat the peelings and all. That afternoon we all set around and ate cucumbers with the peel still on. The salt would not stick very well. You had to lick a spot to make the salt stick. But we ate it.

Here is what you need:

- Please go back to the Pumpkin Pie recipe and copy down the way to make a piecrust.
- Make up two large pie crusts and set them aside.
- I suggest York Apples or any real hard ones like The Old Smokehouse apples.
- Homemade yellow cow butter
- Brown sugar
- Lemon juice -- a tablespoon of vinegar will work if you don't have lemon juice
- Salt
- Cornstarch

Now, here is what you do:

- Turn your oven on to 375 degrees.
- Peel at least one or maybe two quarts of hard sour apples, and slice them into pieces.
- If they are not sour enough, you may need to pour a little lemon juice on them. If you do this, make sure and stir them some to get the lemon on each apple piece.
- Add in three tablespoons of brown sugar and one teaspoon salt. If the apples are runny, sprinkle about 1/2 teaspoon of cornstarch. Mix this up, but don't break up the apples
- Take one of the piecrusts and put it in your pie pan.
- Spoon in the apples, and mound them up high. They will cook down some.
- About every two inches put a large piece of yellow cow butter. No, you cannot use too much!
- Put the other piecrust on top of the apples. Be careful, because the dough will tear easily.
- Once this is done, take a fork and mash both the piecrusts together around the edges.
- Poke holes in the crust with a broom straw to let the steam out. (Grandmother would let me print my name in the crust with a broom straw.)
- Bake for 25 to 35 minutes until the crust is golden brown.

Serving suggestions:

It is best to have pie like this one after a good solid meal. I would suggest pinto beans, cracklin cornbread, baked sweat potatoes, rich yellow cow butter, strong sweet tea and lots of sweet milk.

Eat the pie afterwards, with hot coffee tempered with rich fresh cream. Mom liked to put a scoop of vanilla ice cream on top, too.

Blackberry Cobbler

One year there were more wild blackberries than I had ever seen. There were patches everywhere. Now these were not the town kind of blackberries without briars. These were the country kind with two kinds of briars. One full briar set scratched going into the patch. A second sharper, smaller set, dug into your skin coming out of the patch. The coming out kind had fewer teeth, but they were much stronger. Sometimes they would not turn loose until it thundered. Just like a full-grown snapping turtle.

Daddy said he would give me 50 cents a gallon for every gallon that I picked. Now, it seems like I never had more than two lousy nickels rubbing together in my pocket at one time. So I agreed. For the next two or three weeks, I picked blackberries.

I did not think that it would be right for me to pick the berries on my uncle's hillside. They would have been too easy; those berries were for his family. So I took to walking up the road looking for easy blackberries. I found a lot, and picked many a two-gallon bucket full.

Before you know it Mom said, "No more berries." We had eaten blackberry cobblers, blackberry dumplings, blackberry pies, and bowls of blackberries with fresh cream. And the freezer was full. There was a lot of jelly made, so much so that it would take a truckload of peanut butter to eat it all up.

But berry picking was not finished yet. People like Miss Lorrina who lived right near to us would call and ask me get her 10 gallons.

Mom would set poor old me down in a chair under the oak tree every evening and dig bee stingers and thorns out of me. She pulled off all of the ticks and put Merthiolate on the spots. She daubed on insect bite lotion to slow down the itch. Every day she would say, "You know, you don't need to pick any more blackberries. Those people can pick their own."

You tried to be at the berry patch before the dew lifted. I wanted to be out by 1:00 p.m., because it began getting hot. Daddy said, "You don't want the berries to get too hot."

Fresh, almost-hot blackberry jam -- the kind that is about half berries, half juice, half seeds and sugar -- put on five or six right-out-of-the-oven, hot biscuits with cow butter is very good.

Now I am not trying to run anybody's cooking skills down with this statement. But there are pie makers and there are pie artists. I have seen both! Aunt Tootie was a true Pie Artist. Her pies were pretty to look at, and they smelled all the way to the road. They had a taste that just seemed to stay right with you. They were so good, in fact, that it would send a red-necked boy right back into them briars again and again.

Well, this is the best Momma Ruth could do at remembering how she made a cobbler. Please note the size of the pie. There were seven hungry mouths to feed plus all the kids on the hill.

Here is what you need:

- Two cups of yellow cow butter cut into little pieces
- Two cups of white sugar
- Two cups of water (If your berries are mashed and runny you can use juice rather than water.)
- Three cups of self-rising flour
- 2/3 cup of whole fresh cream
- Four cups of blackberries
- One teaspoon of ground cinnamon

Now, here is what you do:

- Turn on the oven to 350 degrees.
- In a big baking dish, one that will hold at least a gallon, melt about half of the butter and set the dish on the counter.
- In a big mixing bowl pour in the flour and cut in the last of the butter with a knife and fork. Cut the flour until it looks like rice.
- Now pour in the milk and mix until a dough forms, then add in the cinnamon.
- Dump the dough out on a floured place on the counter and knead four or five times.
- Put all of the berries and everything else in the big baking dish.
- Break up the dough into one-inch pieces, and add those to the berries one piece at a time. Kind of stir it into the mixture. (Mom said that you can roll the dough into smallish balls about the size of a sewing thimble, if you like.)
- Put the big dish in the oven and bake about 45 to 50 minutes.

Vinegar Pie

Grandmother and Mom called a Vinegar Pie a "Poor Man's Apple Pie." Momma Ruth said that a Vinegar Pie was a way to use up extra eggs and to have something different to eat. In the spring all the chickens produced more eggs than anyone could eat up. Momma made Vinegar Pie just to have something else to put on the table, not to mention using up all those eggs.

Grandmother made the pies, too. She always had eggs for sale, but it seemed almost no one ever came to buy her eggs. Grandmother's house was just a little off of the beaten path. People wanting fresh homegrown eggs went to other old ladies' homes up and down the ridge, and they could usually sell every egg that was laid. In a pinch those other Old Egg Selling Grandmothers would come by and purchase my grandmother's eggs and pass them off as theirs.

So, those they didn't buy most times went into rich Vinegar Pies. The vinegar gives the pie a slight apple-ish taste. Of course, anything that is mostly butter and eggs is good, but no one makes Vinegar Pie much anymore. It is a piece of antiquity.

Here is what you need:

- Go to the section with the pie dough recipe and make the dough.
- 1/2 cup of butter melted, but not hot
- Four eggs
- 1/4 cup of apple vinegar
- Four tablespoons of all-purpose flour
- One tablespoon of vanilla
- One 9" pie pan

Now, here is what you do:

- Cut the oven on to 325 degrees.
- Put the piecrust in the 9" pie pan.
- Slightly beat the eggs.
- Mix the eggs, butter, sugar, flour, vinegar, and vanilla in a bowl and pour into the pan.
- Bake for one hour.
- Let the pie cool for a few hours before serving it.

A Cake from the Past

When I stop and think about the past, one of the things I can remember Mom and Grandmother making is Mayonnaise Cake. Grandmother said that she did not like to make them much anymore, because it always reminded her of World War ll and hard times. She said that it was a very hard time before the war and real hard times when four of her five sons were gone. All four returned to River Ridge. She told me one time that they just seemed to think that they were going on a trip or a kind of vacation. She said, "I told them that World War I was just plain hard. There was no food unless you could grow it, and some men were gone for years and then some did not come back. Uncle Nelson, the brother that did not go to war, remained on the hill.

Nelson and Aunt Tootie lived in the house just under the hill next to Mom and Dad. Nelson said he had his family to feed, Grandmother's family and Aunt Toot's mother and father, too. Nelson told me that when he and Toot went to Prices Fork to visit, they each carried a bucket and a hoe. They had gardens planted on about every level spot between River Ridge and Prices Fork. "You chopped weeds and picked beans, potatoes and corn both coming and going." From River Ridge to Prices Fork was a five-mile walk. Also, everyone walked. If you had a car, there wasn't any gas. If you did not grow it you did not eat. Food items just weren't to be had. Nelson and Aunt Toot said: "I just do not know how people in towns and cities made it through the war. Out here, we had some land for hogs and gardens."

One of many things that they were short of was Crisco and lard. Mayonnaise has a lot of vegetable oil in it, so they used mayonnaise instead of lard. I asked why they did not use lard in the cakes. In the summer the lard could get real strong. Also, without all the men on the hill there were not as many hogs butchered. Well anyway, in the summer you used mayonnaise in your cakes.

Here is Momma Ruth's and Mamaw's Chocolate Mayonnaise Cake. Momma and I sat at the nursing home, and together we remembered this recipe.

Here is what you need.

- Two cups of regular, unsifted flour
- 2/3 cup of unsweetened cocoa
- 1 1/4 teaspoon of baking powder
- 1/4 teaspoon of baking soda
- Three eggs
- 2/3 cup of white sugar
- One teaspoon of vanilla
- One cup of mayonnaise
- 1/3 cup of water

Now, here is what you do.

- Grease up and flour two cake pans and set them aside.
- Get out two bowls.
- In one put the flour, cocoa, baking soda and baking powder; lightly mix them up.
- In the other bowl put eggs, sugar, vanilla and mix until it is fluffy.
- Now slowly mix in the mayonnaise.
- Add the flour and water and mix until the flour is incorporated and stop mixing.
- Pour into the pans and bake at 350 degrees for about 30 minutes.
- Put on any cake icing you like.

Snow Ice Cream

Back in the day, we got a lot of snow on River Ridge. Mom and I were talking about this a few weeks ago. I said, "When I was a child it seemed like every time it snowed, the snow came up almost to my knees."

Momma answered, "It did, but keep in mind your knees were about six inches off the ground." Now that might just be true. But it did seem to be much deeper. We wore out about anything that would slide over the hill.

I have to admit, I did like sled riding. I had an old sled; it was not a very good one. It spent its summers just leaning on the hog pen. The boards turned brown with age and rot. The runners rusted up browner than the boards. Looking back, that old sled suffered from a lot of neglect. I never once took one bit of care of it. It never even got a good name like Rosebud. It was just an old sled.

With the first sign of snow I headed for the barn and pulled off three or four hay strings from Uncle Shorty's pile. I tied them to the front of the old sled and start dragging it around the yard trying to knock off some of the rust. When I pulled it in the gravels by the mailbox, that shined it up about as quick as anything.

When I finally got the runner slick enough to go over the hill, it would go fast. I think that was because I was fat and weight helped it gain speed. Once you got down the hill you always had that hard walk back to the house. Momma Ruth, I am sure, was watching out the window, because no sooner did I crest the hill than she would take to hollering for me to come in. She always, as regular as a clock ticking, had a big pan of hot chocolate boiling. I would drink down four or five big jars, and I would be off and ready for another trip down the hill.

Once I hit the big walnut tree at the pond and broke the wooden steering lever. Never fear, Elmer looked the situation over and then took his foot and finished breaking the steering lever out. "Well that won't get in the way anymore," he said. I stood in shock for only a second. I jumped on the thing and was gone over the hill again. I just learned to hold the front of the runners to steer.

Another time I jumped on the sled too hard and broke all of the cross braces right in half. Daddy just went to the barn and pulled out a board 2" thick by 18" wide and 36" long. We pulled the sled back together and nailed it. Fat little boys are hard on sleds! The big board added another eight or ten pounds to the total weight of the sled.

Each climb back up the hill was a lot farther than the last and harder, too. My intake of hot chocolate just got greater.

About the time I thought that my little legs would fall off, I would hear Momma calling for me. My fat little legs sprung to life.

I just knew that Momma was outside collecting up the freshest snow she could find. I just knew that she had melted the cream and sugar and mixed some vanilla. She was going to make up some ice cream. And it was always good.

I always liked the snow ice cream. We ate it about it two or three times each winter. That was enough to get it out of my mother's system. We all ate the stuff, even Elmer. The whole time we were eating it Elmer would talk about air pollution coming out of the air when it snowed. He even talked about the radiation falling back to Earth and being caught by the snow. That is why you have got to get the best snow possible.

Here is what you need

- A fat little boy with real big eyes and a round chumboser
- Two gallons of the cleanest snow you can find
- 1/2 pound of brown sugar
- Two cups of cream
- One tablespoon of vanilla
- 1/4 tablespoon of cinnamon (optional)

Now here is what you do:

- In the very biggest mixing bowl you have, add the cream, brown sugar, and vanilla – add the cinnamon too, if you choose to use it. Mix the stuff until it is about to turn into whipped cream.
- Set the bowl out in the snow to cool.
- Go dig up two gallons of the cleanest snow you can find.
- Go get the cream bowl and fill it almost to the top with snow.
- Fold the ingredients together and serve before it melts.

Making Fudge

One of the most fun things we ever did was to make homemade fudge candy. A few things had to be just right for this to happen. It needed to be a warm day followed by a cold night so the fudge could harden, and Daddy needed to be sober enough to make the experience tolerable. That generally meant a cold Saturday in the fall. And everyone needed to be ready to work.

It all started by looking in the kitchen cabinets to see if there was enough sugar, Crisco and cocoa. If there was, I was dispatched to go find up every coal scuttle I could. We then set off to the sawmill hollow where there were a bunch of Shag Bark Hickories. One of them was one giant of a tree. Daddy said that you could make a thousand hammer handles out of it. But, this day we were trying to pick up hickory nuts before the squirrels got them all. We filled up every scuttle we had and start for home. It was about three miles roundtrip.

We took the nuts to the lower end of the lot, below the hog lot on the old, ancient road. Each child was given a good-sized flint rock, a small hammer and a bowl. You set to cracking and digging out the nutmeats. Also, we picked up about a bushel

156

of black walnuts. They were cracked, too, but we kept them separate from the other nuts because they have strong flavors. They are good, but you don't need many.

Daddy was the candy-maker, not Mom. He'd get out a big pan and fill it with water about halfway and set it to boiling. On top of the boiling water he set a second smaller pan. It was a big double boiler of some kind. Into the pan he put a pound or two of butter and Crisco. Once it had melted down and was boiling some, he added in lots of sugar, vanilla and cocoa and took to stirring. I think that we took turns stirring for hours.

No one ever said, "Now, be careful and don't get scalded to death by the two gallons of boiling water." No, I was just told don't stir so fast that you knock the candy mixture out onto the floor.

Mom and Dad took out spoonfuls of the hot candy and slowly pour it through the air and watched it make swirls on top of the other candy. This was done a lot. But finally they said, "It is time for the nuts. Each of you get your bowls out and add in the nuts while we stir."

The mixture was then poured and scraped into a long shallow pan and smoothed out. Daddy carried it outside and set it on a table to harden. I just loved to set in the cold moonlight and watch that stuff harden, knowing that I would get to eat it. It was quiet, and I liked that.

It took all day to make fudge. It was good and I loved the stuff, but, looking back, it was not worth the time and effort. Mom and Daddy just wanted something for me to do and something sweet to eat. Momma Ruth said she and Elmer never did have a recipe for fudge -- they just kept fooling with it until it was right.

Sometimes, if everything had gone well, we would experiment. Once or twice we lined up marshmallows about 1/4 inch apart and poured hot fudge over them. When it cooked, it was like a soft, store-bought candy bar. I liked it when we put whole almonds in the fudge. Really, I just liked it any way Momma and Daddy fixed the stuff.

Bonnets and Apple Butter

You could always tell when apple butter and soap making was coming. Mom, my aunts, and all of the old ladies started looking for their old bonnets. I do not know if it is a rule that old ladies wear bonnets for these activities or not. I think that it is, because when apple butter making was over they promptly threw the bonnets away.

It seemed like on the same day the next fall they started digging through stuff that had not seen the light of day since about this time last year.

The appearance of bonnets was a surefire way of knowing apple butter making is coming. They make new bonnets if the old ones cannot be found. Just imagine women setting around on old cane bottom chairs peeling apples with them bonnets on. The only break from this humorous sight was watching them fighting gnats and swatting at bees while they peeled apples.

Sometimes these ladies would cluster up and talk real quiet-like. I think they were talking about their husbands, because every once in a while they would burst into laughter and say something like, "No, he did not."

159

Once in a while I would say that it would be easier to go inside and use the wood stove, but no one acted like they even heard a word I had said. After apple butter or lard was canned, the copper pot washed and everything put up, you could hear all of them say, "Next year we are going to make the apple butter in the house on the wood stove. I am not wearing that bonnet ever again. It makes me look like a fool."

Most of my job for these activities was cutting firewood and lots of it. Preparation started in July or August. My uncle cut one locust tree per day for the livestock. Cows and horses love the sweet locust leaves. The dead trees lay there all fall drying out. Uncle Shorty cut posts out of the trunk. I split a very large pile of locust wood out of the limbs.

It was a very exacting job. I put pieces of old fence posts on the wood holder and used a buck saw to cut 8-inch sections, just like I did for the wood cook stove, and split them into pieces about the size of a ball bat on the end. I cut all of the limbs up the same way.

I asked why it had to be so exact. Grandmother's answer was simple: "It will give you something to do and keep your mind occupied while we are making apple butter."

One time, I was splitting a piece of wood with an ax. It was frosty cold, but I had not given in to wearing shoes yet. I was putting the locust blocks on the chopping block and cutting them in half. One of the twisted pieces just kept falling off so I leaned it up against the chopping block and held it in place with my bare foot. I hit the wood and it split and so did my big toe. Now there was a cut right down the middle of my toe almost to the bottom where the quick starts. I was screaming and running for help.

Mom and Grandmother come to see what all the racket was. They looked my toe over. "Does it hurt?" they asked in unison.

"Yes!" I screamed. I have always thought that was a dumb question – does it hurt?

They started the treatment: soap and water, a great big glob of Raleigh Salve and poultice of some kind of herbs. They tied it up with an old clean white cloth torn from a bed sheet and told me to put my shoes on. They sent me back to finish my job. It did hurt, but I knew that there was no reason to complain about it. There was no doctor within an hour's drive, and there was apple butter to be made.

I heard one of them say as I left the kitchen: "Now, look at that bloody mess on the floor and with all of this work to do. There is always something extra to do."

I guess they did care if I was hurting, but not too much. If they did they were not going to let on any. There was apple butter to be made.

The first day, Mom, my aunts and Grandmother would start peeling and slicing apples into large pans. After they had about seven or eight bushels peeled and sliced up, they inspected the bright copper kettle. The next morning about 4:00 a.m. or earlier, Grandmother started a fire under the pot, and then began dumping in the small bucket of water or some applesauce she had made the day before. When it got warm she added a few of the sliced apples. The process was set in motion and would go nonstop all day and up into the night.

When she woke me up, we ate butter biscuits and fried apples and drank good coffee. I had special coffee back then -- three or four parts milk and fresh cream and one part coffee. But I liked it.

Before anyone else got up and out of bed, we stirred them apples, real slow and steady. Stir too slowly or stop and the apple butter would stick or burn. Stir too fast and you would splash out the apple butter. This went on from way before daylight until about dark.

When the apples cooked down more slices would be added. I kept the apples at a very low boil for many hours. If a bee or fly got in the apple butter I tried to fish it out. If I could not get him I just stirred him to the bottom where he got cooked too. My mom, aunts and grandmother would jump in and stir a little while and taste. If time seemed to be getting away from us, they built a big fire in the wood stove in the kitchen to cook raw apples down some before adding them to the apple butter pot. Just to speed us up.

While they did the important part of tasting, I was dispatched to get more wood and stir some more. I was the best taster, I think. The closer the apple butter got to being ready someone would come out of the house carrying a tray of hot biscuits, yellow cow butter and plates. Fresh-perked coffee just set on a rock by the fire. The coffee smelled as good as the apple butter.

Everyone got a biscuit, a spoon and a little dish, even me. Every once in a while they would add sugar, cinnamon and occasionally cloves. You dipped out a little hot fresh apple butter onto your plate. Then you set around and ate little spoonfuls and smacked your lips some.

It looked like a bunch of wine tasters in bonnets. You could eat some on your biscuits or just eat it straight -- anyway you liked. I always thought that the "on the biscuit" taste was the most telling. Aren't you going to eat it on a biscuit with butter anyway? Eating apple butter without a biscuit is kind of like washing your feet with your socks still on.

Then all the ladies started suggesting what spices were needed. Some said just a little more cinnamon, or cloves, more sugar, possibly another pinch of salt and so on until everyone was satisfied.

I think I like the homemade butter biscuits most of all. I have been known to eat the clove-flavored apple butter, but there will always be a weak spot in my chumboser for the cinnamon. Daddy said that he was like a cow and had three or four stomachs, one of which he thought was the chumboser. I must have one of them, too.

During the week leading up to apple butter making everyone had washed quart jars. Once the apple butter was made it had to be canned. Sometime in the late evening it was deemed to now be apple butter and was carefully ladled into the jars, carried into the house and put in the canners. It was hard work, but it was fun. It would also make you sleep real good and sound.

POUR IT ON!

The Warm Taste of Almond Brandy

As I tell you this I want you to keep in mind that the only thing that can make me sicker than the smell of spoiled sauerkraut is the smell of old almonds dropped into a one-gallon jar of moonshine. In the fall of 1968, at the ripe old age of 17, I found myself at a hippy party out on the cliffs behind Prices Fork. I found this bottle of moonshine on a bookcase near a fine setting chair. On closer observation, I discovered the bottom of the jar was covered with about one inch of almonds. I think they were put in there to make the moonshine taste like almond brandy or something.

"How the hell did I know?" you might ask. Well, I truly did not know. You see I had never tasted real almond brandy, or even seen any like this for that matter. But being a true Appalachian American, I just knew lots of things. Also my experience as a coal miner had started my education on all things related to moonshine. So, I instinctively knew what them hippies were trying to do.

I took a long, slow drink of the shine. When I swallowed I thought my tongue and throat were going to burn off. It took about half of my Pepsi Cola to cool this stuff off. I wondered if

I was to set the shine on fire, would the flame burn blue? My throat was hot enough to burn blue. Right from the start it tasted bad; long about midnight it was a fine brew and getting to tasting better, whatever it was. Others also helped it along too. But I must be truthful here -- my partners were not as dedicated to this jar as I was.

When I got near to the bottom I took a fork and dug out the almonds and ate every one. A very short time later we were encouraged to leave. Strongly encouraged!

Pretty soon I was sicker than anyone ever was in this whole world. Of this I am sure. Anyone sicker would have just died and got it over with, but I was too hardheaded, I reckon.

The next morning I rushed home for two things. First, I grabbed the newspaper from the box and flipped it to the obituaries as fast as I could. As sick as I was, there was a strong possibility that my demise would be listed in the obituaries. I figured it had been delivered within the last few hours, so the information was very accurate.

I was not listed anywhere in the obituaries. That means that as bad as I was, I was going to get better, one of these days. I just had to wait this hangover out.

The other thing I needed was a brine pickle or two. So, to my uncle's cellar I go. I dig into the crock of salt brine pickles. I take out two. I did just like I had seen the men do. I went to the cistern and pumped water over them to wash off the slime. I set one on the cistern cover and just started eating it. I grabbed the second one before I had any time to think about it. After a second or two of thought, I might have chosen death over the second salt brine pickle.

The pickles worked like a charm. Why, in less than three days I could keep food down, and I could go out in the daytime without my eyes hurting. Within a week my stomach and body was not hurting anymore and I could taste food again. P.S. I swore off almond brandy.

Here is what you need:

- One gallon of high quality corn liquor (that has passed the blue flame test)
- Two pounds of plain, roasted, unsalted almonds. (They ought to be brown-skinned.)
- A one gallon mason jar and a clean lid

Now, here is what you do:

- Drink out about two inches of the corn liquor.
- Slowly pour in the almonds.
- Screw on the lid rather tight and set the jar in the back closet out of sight for two or three months or until some special occasion comes along.

Sometimes a special occasion for Daddy was next Saturday morning. The start of International Potato Week and Old Spike's (Stanley's dog's) birthday were often celebrated on River Ridge. You see, some jars did last until a special occasion.

You can add other flavoring to corn liquor, too. I have added dried apricots, dried peaches and even dried plums (notice I did not say prunes). I have even added fresh fruit such as strawberries, blackberries, peach slices and raspberries. The dried fruit works the best. Strawberries work well, too.

Here is just one more little bit of information. My dad and his brothers all rode together to the moonshiner's to get their corn licker. They wanted to test its purity first. A small amount was poured out into a jar lid and set on fire. If the stuff burnt blue, it was good stuff and they bought a lot. When I was along I never saw anything that was not deemed, "among the highest quality they ever saw. Damn that is good ain't it?" When I would sneak and taste the stuff it burned my mouth and throat. High quality or poor quality, it was just bad stuff.

Even today there are places that I visit where I am offered small tastes right out of a half-gallon jar. It is as clear as any water I ever drank. When I swallow, it is hot as any gasoline, and quite capable of burning off a fever blister, too. No sir, some things never change. Today, we pass the jar from one to another, and everyone takes a drink. We all like a taste of good clean well-made corn licker. Well, except me; I like a well-chilled Chardonnay or Sauvignon Blanc. But I do tend to sacrifice my body for the group.

Fruit of the Vine

When I got grown, one of my most favorite jobs in the entire world was working in a winery. At the time I had no idea this experience would stick with me the rest of my life. Like many things in life, this opportunity happened by accident. It was 1980. I was going to college and broke as a convict. I still did not have two nickels to my name. I needed a job and just about anything would do.

On one of my horticulture field trips from Virginia Tech, the whole class visited MJC Vineyard in the Roanoke Valley. After the tour, Dr. Carl Herford, the owner of MJC, asked if anyone wanted to work the next weekend. "If yes, show up on Saturday morning." Well, I showed up and stayed for about three and a half years.

Working around wine should have been nothing new to me. You see, I grew up on wine. There was your homemade Concord grape wine. About everyone made this, but it was one of my very own mother's specialties. Then there was your homemade dandelion wine. Uncle Shorty made seven or eight gallons of this each year. Once in a while someone would find a vine or two of fox grapes. This, too, was made into wine.

Why, we even made mulberry wine. If you even thought that it could be fermented, the Lyttons tried it. Mulberry wine was very sweet and had a light red color about it. Early in the summer it was the local redneck hit.

Mr. Clyde Wilburn, one of our neighbors, made mulberry wine in two or three large crocks. Daddy and all of his brothers went regularly to Clyde's for wine. They told Mom, Grandmother and Toot they were going to help Clyde catch a bull or to cut (castrate) his pigs – "I hear they are getting out and it is time to get that job done." Sometimes they went to help plane a piece of lumber. They would tell this story over and over, sometimes twice a day. Now, you tell me just how many times do you have to castrate pigs or plane the same lumber? Who in the world do you think they were fooling?

You could always tell when Mr. Clyde was into the wine -- he would rinse his mouth out with gas. Yes, gas right out of the lawnmower gas can. He just turned up the little can and took a mouthful and gargled like it was mouthwash. Mr. Clyde did not want his wife, Miss Lorinna, to know that he was drinking. I did this only once. I thought that I would choke to death, and Daddy smelled the gas on my breath and told me to stay out of the mulberry wine. "That trick only fooled Miss Lorinna," he said.

While I never saw Uncle Nelson make wine, he drank his share and someone else's too. He liked Old 97, Thunderbird, Sly Fox and something called Muscatel. At one time, if he drank it, so did I. All of these exotic, unknown store-bought beverages were more commonly called "old head bust." I can testify that "old head bust" was a well-earned and fitting name. I never once saw anybody drinking anything with a cork. A cork was far too troublesome. They wanted a screw-top cap for the convenience and quickness of opening. The screw cap only had to work one time. I don't recall many wine bottles ever being recapped. Taste, aroma and bouquet were unknown words on River Ridge. But River Ridge men did speak of volume, availability and location of the bottle.

You can see I was well suited to work in the vineyard. My first day I never got near any wine. It was early winter, and the leaves had already fallen. For the first few weeks I dug up bare-rooted, three-year-old grapevines and put them into bundles of 25. The bundles went into a big cooler for storage.

Some time later, Dr. Herford asked me to drive to a vineyard in Northern Virginia and deliver the vines and bring back a pallet of new wine bottles. What I found was the largest vineyard / wine bottle storage facility I had ever seen, -- seven or eight men harvesting grapes from ten acres of producing vines, a warehouse with bottles of wine stacked to the ceiling, and a working bottling line. I had only read about such things. Seven or eight men trimming vines, tying up cordons, and some rolling up Christmas wreaths. There were stacks of wine bottles floor to ceiling, and to my amazement an honest-to-goodness bottling line.

Over the next few years I learned to trim and trellis vines, for both MJC and two other smaller vineyards. My hands and arms ached from the trimming. The carpal tunnel syndrome I have today may have started with grape trimming. But, it was an important job and I loved doing it. I found that I was fast and good at it. I somehow seemed to understand the trellising system and knew how to maximize the light infiltration and airflow. I learned to be happy for good spring and summer rains and how to curse the late August rains that came with hurricanes. I have seen great fruit with wonderful potential fill with too much water and split, thereby turning into only passable fruit in a matter of hours.

I learned how to identify different grape diseases and how to treat them. It is funny—even today I think about spray schedules and downy and powdery mildew and the chemicals used to treat them. I also think back fondly about walking through vineyards suckering each vine (removing the unwanted new growth from the main stem). The thing I valued most wasn't necessarily drinking the wine, but learning about it. Still, I have to admit learning it with a glass in hand is a lot more fun!

Words like Seyval, Vidal, Chambourcin, Chardonnay, Chancellor, Pinot, Merlot, Cabernet, Riesling, racking and oxidation became part of my vocabulary. I learned to taste the wine before I drank it, you know, like a red-necked boy always shakes up the milk before he drinks it, just to mix up the milk and the cream. I grew to appreciate the difference between each grape's flavor and the smell of each wine. I thought that it was great to go to work in the morning and find the first thing to be done was set down and taste seven or eight wines. Wines that were opened the day before could be oxidized and needed to be disposed of. If they were still good, I served them to customers. Some days, Carl and I would set down in the winemaker's lab and taste different wines and different blends. Each day I learned more about what constitutes wine quality. Before this, the only quality I was interested in was the volume of alcohol—how much there is and where is it. Taste was of little importance. Sounds familiar, doesn't it?

We made the red wine in an old car garage. I guess there were 25 or 30 open blue plastic barrels. Once the clusters were de-stemmed, I carried the juice, seeds, and pulp in five-gallon buckets to fill each barrel. Then someone put a piece of cheesecloth on the top to keep the flies and bugs out. About every two hours, day and night, for a week I removed the cheesecloth and punched down the floating skins and seeds. There were no fans or windows. I later learned that each year people died from carbon monoxide poisoning from fermenting red grapes. Well, I never did get sick. I guess that I am just tough, not too bright, just tough. And, our scale of production was small.

For the white wine—Duchess, Chardonnay, and Seyval —we picked the clusters and sent them straight to a press. The raw juice was pumped into 1000-gallon plastic containers. MJC had four of these containers in a large air-conditioned room where the temperature never got above 50 degrees.

This same room housed our bottling line. We bottled and

put labels on by hand. It took about four minutes to fill six bottles of wine. Today that seems so very slow, but it sure was fast for me. If someone came to the tasting room, you stopped what you were doing and waited on customers.

There were two kinds of visitors that frequented MJC Vineyards. Sometimes they were in the same car. One of the funniest customers that ever came to the vineyard was Uncle Shorty, who appeared one afternoon after I had been working there for more than a year. He could not believe there was such a place. I gave him the standard tour. When we got to the white wine building, the one with four 1000-gallon tanks of white wine, Shorty just kind of petted the big tanks like they were real big dogs. He looked over at me and asked if I had "just one big straw." Shorty did not like much of the wine. He said that it was sour, "something that only a spaghetti bender would drink." But, he did like the Duchess Wine, a lighter, sweeter wine made from the "Duchess Grape," an American grape.

Shorty bought a bottle and headed for home. After about 15 minutes he came back up the driveway; he was mad and talking right loud. "You gave me something with a damn cork. How in the hell do you expect me to get at the stuff?" He handed me the bottle, and the cork looked like Woody Woodpecker had been trying to remove it. I asked how this happened, and he informed me that he had been setting on the side of the road, chipping away on it with a bent nail. I opened it with a corkscrew, and he said, "Who in the hell would want such a thing with a cork anyway!"

Another local who came for a visit was as skilled a consumer of alcohol as they come. He walked the whole vineyard and winery with me, asked more questions than anyone ever had, and looked at every vine, the clean soil under the vines, the tractor and the sprayer. We even reviewed the chemicals in the shed, and talked about what pests they were used to control. When he saw the large containers of wine, he echoed Shorty: "That is a lot of wine, and you would need a long straw and lot of time to drink all of that." He tasted everything we had and made some of the same comments as Shorty, but he had come to see the vineyard, while Shorty came to see the wine. I think they both liked what they saw.

One day, a very rough-looking man with a truck full of bear hounds came to the vineyard and introduced himself to me as a professional bear hunter and an amateur coon hunter. He wanted to trade fresh-caught bear paws for wine, four paws for two bottles. When I told him "No Trade," he was kind of offended. But, I did ask him to start coon hunting in the vineyards. The raccoons would walk down the cordon and partially eat a cluster and move on to another one.

One very hot day in late August, not one person had been to the vineyard all day, the spraying was done and mowing a week away, so I was caught up. I saw a dust cloud coming up the driveway, and lo and behold, an old friend pulled in with his young son. I poured each of them a glass -- one got wine, the other apple juice. We walked all over the place, talked about wine, mostly talked about happenings since we had last seen

177

each other and finally settled in the shade of the vines. As the evening wore on the number of bottles grew. My friend decided that he needed cigarettes. I truly explained that we needed a little coffee before he went anywhere.

Before you know it we were driving down the valley very fast. I explained that there was a curve fast approaching known to be banked the wrong way, and at this speed we couldn't make this turn. I asked his son to put on his seat belt, and I tightened it up real tight. I put mine on, too, and pulled it down right tight. We wrecked in the turn. No one was hurt. The boy and I were left hanging upside down. We both dropped with a thud when the seat belts released. When everything was said and done, I was made out to be the one at fault and I was not even driving. I learned to be a little more insistent where drunks are concerned. I never ever had another sip of wine at work, other than the job-related tasting in the mornings and afternoons, or when no one but me was around. I guess I was somewhat at fault. I knew that cigarettes are not the healthiest thing. They can give you lung cancer. Car wrecks aren't too healthy, either.

One morning Carl Herford asked me fill in for him at a professional wine tasting. A group of faculty from Virginia Tech was meeting in Blacksburg. MJC Vineyards was to be the entertainment. He had agreed to conduct a sit-down wine tasting, so I chilled some wines in coolers and opened others to put into Carl's fancy decanters to let breathe. I loaded up all the wine glasses we had, white tablecloths, and the wine and put on my only suit. I looked the part of a wine sommelier (the little French wine server). I set off. I had no earthly idea what I doing, but I did it anyway. One of my past professors in attendance noted that if I had paid as much attention in his class as I had to winemaking, I would have been a genius. I have participated in many wine events since.

One of the hardest jobs was delivering wine. Carl had bought a used one-ton pickup from the Norfolk and Western Railroad. The thing was just a little past worn out when he got it. It had big holes on the seat with springs sticking up and eight-ply tires, plus no power steering with a three-speed on the column. Yes, a big bright orange cream puff. Each time, before I got in, I checked the oil. Often the engine needed a few quarts – yes, a few quarts. I made sure that there was at least a case of real thick and real cheap oil on hand at all times, for the old truck liked the stuff.

Each month I made deliveries in this thing. Each month I inspected it from bumper to bumper. In those days each winery did its own advertisement, promotion and shipping. One day we would make a list of each wine order. Then, Carl and I would stack the bottles on the floor of the winery and label each box. We started with the restaurants closest to the Roanoke Valley. They went in the truck first. For example, The Hotel Roanoke was the first on, near the cab. Deliveries to Virginia Beach went on last, near the tailgate.

The whole loaded truck had to be driven to Virginia Beach, since deliveries started there. Do not ask me why; this is just the way we did it. Carl was not from Blacksburg, but he had lived in Appalachia long enough to learn to do everything the hardest possible way. In true Appalachian fashion, the hard way is always the best way. It has always worked for me.

So on a Sunday night at 10:00 or 11:00 p.m., me and the big orange smoking truck started out for Virginia Beach. In the early morning as restaurants opened, I went from one restaurant to the next, dropping off wine and collecting money. I also kept about five or six bottles of extra wine in the front. "You never know, you might get lost and run across a new restaurant that would like to carry our wine," Carl explained.

This was a true statement. Just on a lark or just to see what would happen, one morning I stopped at the Hotel Roanoke and introduced myself to the manager and the head chef. I told them my position in MJC Vineyards. I gave the chef a bottle of our Paris Mountain Seyval Blanc. I said, "I like it with salmon, shellfish and baked chicken."

"Do you now?" he answered. The next month the Hotel Roanoke was a regular stop. There, I would set down like a real wine expert and talk wine and food. I ate well and enjoyed wine in proper, American Boy fashion. Yes, I liked that phase of my life.

I also made a monthly run to the Virginia Alcohol warehouse in Richmond. These wines were shipped to every ABC Store in Virginia. We carefully selected the best-looking bottles, the ones with very straight labels. By hand we placed a gold foil on the top of each bottle. The bottles then were very carefully placed in wine boxes by girls, who Carl said were more careful than boys or us.

On one occasion, I got a call in the middle of the night from Carl. The State Alcohol people in Richmond had called him. The MJC Vineyard wines were exploding in the warehouse. There was one hell of a mess. I got out of bed, drove to the vineyard and picked up everything that I could find to clean with and put it all in the big yellow truck. I loaded up Carl, too.

We drove to Richmond and found one of the biggest messes there ever was! Bottles were still popping while we were cleaning up. The wine was not "still," but going through what is called a "malolactic secondary fermentation." We loaded each bottle by hand back onto the yellow truck and brought it back to the Roanoke Valley. The next delivery was just whatever in the hell we could find, and it went the way it was! No fine girl labor was used on this shipment.

At the time I worked for MJC Vineyards, the first Dirty Dancing movie – you know, the one with Jennifer Gray and Patrick Swayze -- was being made at the Mountain Lake Resort. At the time, MJC Vineyards made a special wine called Mountain Lake Seyval for the resort. People up there loved this wine. During the filming of the movie I made a delivery every week. Also, the resort people brought hotel guests and actors to the vineyard for tours and tastings.

Carl Herford asked me one afternoon who came from

Mountain Lake for the tour. I said that there were seven or eight people.

"Did Patrick Swayze or Jennifer Gray come? Did you get pictures?"

"I am very sorry to say, I have no clue."

Carl said, "No matter. A low-budget picture filmed at Mountain Lake that focuses on dancing is never going to be watched by anyone. Who are Patrick Swayze and Jennifer Gray anyway?"

Now that all of this is in the past, I can bet that both actors came to MJC, and I did not even know it. I did not get one picture for the wall and no autograph for me, either. My contact with famous people came and went, and I did not even know it had happened.

In 2007 a movie film crew came from England to make a television show entitled "Dirty Dancing, the Times of our Lives." They rounded up about everyone they could think of that had ever been around the original movie. I, too, was rounded up. When I told them my experiences with the original movie, they very politely turned away. No, now that I think back on it they ran away from me. One minute we were talking; the next second I was talking to myself. My second brush with fame came and went too. Who knows? Possibly my third encounter will reveal all my pent-up acting talent, and everyone will be real sorry they did not make a star out of me.

As I visited other Virginia vineyards, sometimes I dropped off stuff. Other times I picked up supplies. Often the owners and managers would ask me to taste their wine from the barrel or from a large tank. "What do you honestly think?" they would ask.

Please note, this is asked of every professional, not just me. Still, here I was being included in this professional winemaking fraternity. It made me feel like Lance Compton. I think that was the man's name on "Falcon Crest," wasn't it? Well, we do look a lot alike anyway; sometimes people still get us confused. I can bet it's a real problem for him, too, being confused with me and all.

Sometimes people sent me an unlabeled bottle of wine with a handwritten note: "Taste this and let me know that you think." That, too, was fun. Carl said I had a good palate. Even today, 20 years later, some of the older winemakers remember me. They offer me a tasting from the backroom. I taste wine from tanks and barrels. "What would you do with this?" Their winemaker has long since made up his or her mind, but I do enjoy being asked.

Yes, I do like wine! I like every aspect of wine, mostly the drinking of it.

On the next page is Momma Ruth's Concord Grape Wine Recipe, guaranteed to cure what ails you or make you sick as a dog. It has been my experience, that it will do both!

Here is what you need:

- In a three-gallon crock or jar, put two gallons of Concord Grapes right off the vine behind the house.
- Add two quarts of water
- Then pour in four cups of sugar

Now, here is what you do:

- Cover the top with cheesecloth. Put the crock in a back closet out of the way. Every time you think about it, carefully push the grapes down under the juice. Let them set for two to three weeks for all of the grapes to settle to the bottom..
- Now mash the grapes with a potato masher.
- Strain the juice by pouring it through cheesecloth.
- Catch all the juice and measure it right close. There ought to be very close to two gallons.
- Pour the juice back into the crock and add two cups of sugar.
- Let the juice stand for two weeks and pour it through cheesecloth again. This will get all the scum off the top of the wine. Add another cup of sugar.
- Let it stand for another week and strain it again and add a cup of sugar.
- Strain the juice again and pour it into quart jars. Do not put the lid on tight.
- It might take a few months for the wine to finish working.

EAT WHAT YOU HAVE
LOVE WHAT YOU EAT

Waste Not, Want Not
Chowchow

Chowchow was waste product from the fall garden to many, but to those of us living on River Ridge it was a most wonderful and cherished fall food. You might even call it an Appalachian condiment. Fortunately, I never had to answer the question, "Just how would you eat your pinto beans without chowchow?" For me, it might have been as bad as trying to eat pinto beans without cornbread. For some, chowchow was one of the poor man's foods you ate, but just did not talk much about it. I heard it once called a "real soul food." That I do not know about. My scope of things only reached as far as the edge of River Ridge.

Today, I find it right humorous to see jars of chowchow on the shelves of gourmet stores and gift shops. I see my mother and father and aunts and uncles walking the weed-choked garden looking for the last vegetables of the season. Now I sometimes see a pint jar that will sell for $3.00 or even $4.00. Once up the Blue Ridge Parkway I saw a shelf with eight or ten kinds of chowchow. During my youth, if you were living on River Ridge the type of vegetables put into cast-iron kettles might vary some, but there was just one purpose! Chowchow was for pinto beans, and just as important as strong onions.

Toward the early fall, everyone was in the process of laying the garden by for another season. The potato bin in the cellar was filled to the top; the rest of the potatoes were buried in the garden on the side nearest to the house. Sauerkraut had been made, and all of the remaining good solid heads of cabbage had been buried, too. But something had to be done with the remaining cabbage. As you looked across the garden you discovered there were lots of vegetables left. Most were a little past maturity, but with a little thought and hard work they could be made into something that could be eaten. Grandmother said, "There are still empty jars in the cellar. If it gets cold this winter, we will have food to eat. If it stays warm, all you will be out is a day's work."

When it was still a few weeks before frost, with buckets to the garden everyone went. The goal was to pick anything that looked like it could be eaten. It did not matter if the corn was as hard as Chinese arithmetic, or if the cucumbers were a little too big, or if the cabbage heads had busted. Green tomatoes were fine, as well. Everything was brought to the big table in the back yard at Grandmother's. There it was sorted. The really bad stuff went to the hogs, but the rest was washed and chopped up real small.

The vegetables most often used were cabbage, green tomatoes, corn, onions, carrots, cucumbers, and bell peppers. But here is an important part to know. If you had lots of old corn, you made corn chowchow; if there were lots of peppers, you made pepper chowchow. It did not matter what you had; the important thing was you had something!

Our family chopped the vegetables one day and cooked them the next. We used three or four coleslaw shredders to work up 10 or 15 old heads of cabbage. Vegetable pieces needed to be about a 1/4 inch across. We put everything into a galvanized bathtub, sometimes two tubs. Once we'd worked a few handfuls of salt through the mixture, we covered the tubs with an old bed sheet to keep the flies out. The stuff looked a lot like compost, and before long it took to smelling, too.

The next morning, I'd get up very early with Grandmother to start the fire. Soon someone would come out of the house with hot biscuits and apple butter. About all you have to do is let the chowchow boil for a minute or two and simmer for about an hour and then it's ready to can. The steam off of the cast-iron kettle will clean out your sinuses to the point that air goes back up into places it has not gone in weeks. You know you are on the right track. My family canned gallons of chowchow each year; you see, we ate a lot of pinto beans. You may not be going to eat pinto beans more than once or twice a week, so you won't need so much.

My poor old mother had to set and scratch her head on the chowchow recipe. Mom now lives in a nursing home. When I visit and ask her about the old recipes and cooking methods, all of the old ladies just come a-rolling in their wheelchairs to add in their two cents worth. So now, I need to be real honest here; there is some kind of a way to make a small batch. If you want the straight of it, you make a trip to any nursing home, holler out and they will come rolling.

Mom made a second type of chowchow she called pepper relish. Daddy always planted more than 100 bell pepper plants. You needed them for stuffed peppers, some to eat everyday, and some for Mom's pepper relish. We kids ate pepper relish biscuits and carried relish sandwiches to school. They smelled good and tasted even better.

A strange thing happened one day. I mistakenly put red pepper relish in with pinto beans instead of chowchow. I was going to pitch the beans into the hog slop bucket. Mom stopped me: "The beans cost money. You eat them, and it will help you think next time." Well, I ate the beans and they were good. From then on I kind of alternated my chowchow and pepper relish. Life is good sometimes. Now I had a whole new food that I could enjoy.

The recipe on the next page, though, is for the sweet type of regular chowchow. Reduce the sugar and add in more vinegar to make the sour kind.

Here is what you need:

- Two quarts of cabbage shredded really small
- Two average-size onions chopped up small
- One or two red or green bell peppers
- One ear of hard sweet corn
- Two or three tablespoons of salt – salt to your taste
- Three cups of vinegar
- 1 1/2 cups of white sugar
- 2 1/2 teaspoons of dry mustard
- One teaspoon of turmeric
- One teaspoon of dry ginger
- Two teaspoons of black peppercorns
- Two teaspoons of celery seeds
- Two teaspoons of mustard seeds
- One teaspoon of coriander (This is optional. Mom said Grandmother really liked it, so I 'm telling you, too.)
- If you have fresh garlic you can chop up five or six cloves, but this, too, is optional.

Now here is what you do:

- Chop up all of the vegetables and work in salt.
- Let the vegetables set overnight in a cool place – at least 8 hours.
- When you get ready to cook the chowchow, dip the vegetables out of the dishpan with a slotted spoon – or tip up the dishpan over the sink and drain off some of the water.
- Put everything in a 2-gallon pan.
- Mix in all of the herbs, spices and other stuff.
- Stir it a minute to make sure the seasonings are incorporated and let it stand for 15 or 20 minutes. According to my mother, this will get everything working.
- Slowly bring the mixture up to a boil. Let it boil one or two minutes, and then simmer for 15 minutes. It is now ready to be eaten or canned.

Serving suggestions:

Chowchow and beans go together like shoes and socks. I do not care if you have butter beans or October beans – you need chowchow. You need a deep bowl filled with beans. You cover the top of the bowl with a thick layer of black pepper followed by a large spoonful or two of fresh chopped green onions. Lastly, carefully place two rounded-up spoonfuls of chowchow right in the center of the bowl. This is best done at the table because you do not want the chowchow to sink into the beans until you start eating.

What you are after here is the proper Appalachian Presentation. Sometimes, plain food needs care, too. All Appalachian Americans think about their pinto beans.

It is important to eat chowchow the right way. It is not a main course or anything, but is as important to serving pinto beans as streaked salt-cured fat meat. It is, believe me.

You need a tall glass of sweet tea, coleslaw, cornbread with cracklin, lots of onions, and yellow cow butter. That is all that is needed. But if there is a little leftover cottage cheese, now would be a great time to set it out.

Cut your cornbread slice in half while it is hot and add a large chunk of yellow cow butter. Turn the cornbread up on its top so the butter can melt in.

Get yourself a large bowl of pinto beans; you know the kind that cooled down all day and are thick. Cover the beans with black pepper, onions and chowchow as I explained above. Do not go and mix it up. Just eat your way through it and enjoy.

Pinto Beans, Long Shop Style

When I was little, Daddy would sing:

Beans, beans, good for the liver.

The more you eat the more you shiver.

The more you shiver, the more you shake.

It will make you meaner than a rattlesnake.

Pinto beans were the mainstay of our diet. We ate beans with greens. Beans and cornbread went with potatoes. If we cooked it, we ate beans with it and loved it.

Also, notice the volume of beans cooked. Two pounds of dry beans today would feed an army, but not on River Ridge. In our family you needed two gallons of beans for a meal. Also, we did buy bags of pinto beans –beans we had scooped out of a barrel.

Here is what you need:

- A two-gallon stew pot
- Two pounds of dry pinto beans
- A large piece of salt-cured fat meat
- Salt and pepper
- Chopped onions

Now, here is what you do:

- Wash the pinto beans two times.
- In the largest bowl you have, put the beans on to soak covered with at least three inches of water. They are going to swell up a lot.
- Soak the beans over night.
- Put a piece of salt-cured fat meat in a two-gallon stew pot.
- Rinse off the pinto beans and put them in the stew pot, too.
- Put in 1/2 teaspoon of pepper and 1 teaspoon of salt. Be real careful with the salt – mindful of the fat meat.
- Add cold water. Cover the beans with six inches of water. (Biscuits or cornbread sop up a lot of water.)
- Set the beans to boiling. Once they boil set the pan on the cool side of the cook stove for the remainder of the day. If you are using an electric stove, cut the temperature back to simmer for the remainder of the day.

Serving suggestions:

Pinto beans do require fresh chowchow and lots of green onions. If you are eating your beans cold, you need a dash of vinegar. If you are feeling a little more daring a shake of Texas Pete will do the trick.

Fresh right out of the oven cornbread is needed. Hot or cold biscuits can do, too. Plenty of yellow cow butter is a must!

Now, here is another suggestion for you. Hot yeast rolls. Put two hot buttered rolls in the bottom of your bowl and cover them with pinto beans. Cover the beans with chowchow. No matter how you serve the beans you are going to want coleslaw. Maybe some sauerkraut would work well here. Sweet tea is good, too.

Little Miss Muffet Sat on Her Tuffet Eating Her Curds and Whey

Growing up on River Ridge we learned to eat everything! I know that I have said that more than once, but it is true. I do not think it was because we were poorer than others. I think it was because the Depression taught my Grandmother to scrape and scrounge for everything my father and his siblings ate. During the 1920s and 1930s raising ten children on her own must have been an unimaginable job, but Grandmother managed somehow. She had to use everything.

The Depression had a tremendous influence on my family and all of the people on River Ridge. Mod Snider once said, "If you were lucky enough to have a dollar often there wasn't anything to buy." At the same time others made the comment, "If you had a dollar you had better keep it hidden or you wouldn't have it long." For sure, the "hard times" were an education for everyone on River Ridge.

I was born well after the Depression, in 1951 to be exact. In my day everyone had a job that wanted one. But my father's

195

experiences and education in the school of hard knocks received during the "hard times" stayed part of everything my family did. Everyone remembered the hard times, and there were no pleasant memories either. Sometimes I grew very tired of the expression, "Well, boy, you had better eat that. This winter you will think back on it and wish you had eat that. It may taste bad, but it is a hell-of-a-lot better than a snow ball."

In my very earliest remembering, everyone up and down River Ridge had a milk cow. You could not go anywhere overnight, because you had to milk the cows. Some families had three or four cows. As for us, right there on the home place, Uncle Shorty had a Guernsey and a Jersey. We had one and Uncle Nelson had one. Each cow often produced one or two gallons of milk each milking. So the one food we always had was milk. We all drank at least one large glass of milk at each meal. To say the least, I have very strong bones and very hard teeth.

Milk cows got human names too. They were even spoken of as humans. "'Old Betsy' is on top of her milk. Why, she gave two zinc buckets full this morning." Uncle Shorty's Jersey named "Brownie" yielded at least two zinc buckets morning and evening. This was good! "Flower" was mostly light brown in color, but she had a white patch on her sides that resembled a flower. She was a Guernsey who gave a bucket and a half of yellow milk morning and night.

We used every drop of milk every kind of way you could think of. In our house we had two or three crocks in the refrigerator at all times. One crock was for the morning milking; the second was for the evening milking. As the milk cooled the cream came to the top and was skimmed off and put into the third crock. The cream would be made into butter. Now, Flower did not yield as much milk, but people talked about the milk. Locals called Flower's milk "That Golden Guernsey Milk." It was as yellow as corn. We loved the stuff. It did not taste as rich as Brownie's, but the color was different, so different that company unfamiliar with fresh, unpasteurized milk would not drink it. "That milk just ain't natural." We drank it and just loved the butter and cottage cheese.

Milk has two parts, the fat and the whey. Unpasteurized milk or "raw milk" will separate into layers. The lighter weight, the fat part—"the cream"—will rise to the top of the jar. When it's taken off, what's left is thinner looking white fluid, "the whey," mostly protein. The cream was made into whipped cream and butter. The whey was made into buttermilk.

We called the white stuff that was left skim milk or "Blue John." Momma or Grandmother would leave a small amount of the cream in the crock for drinking milk. During the night the milk would separate again. So each time you poured a glass of milk, the milk jug had to be shaken vigorously to mix cream and Blue John into good drinking milk or sweet milk.

There was no way we could drink up all the milk the cows produced, so it seemed like we were always making butter and cottage cheese. Elmer said more than once, "What you can't drink, you got to eat." And we did. Momma would set a three-gallon crock beside the warm stove and fill it with all the unused whole milk. Once the milk came to room temperature or, more accurately, the temperature beside the wood stove, she added in one or two tablespoons of vinegar to the warm milk and gave it quick stir. Within an hour the curds started to form. Soon Momma and Mamaw would pour the stuff in the crocks through a sheet of cheesecloth.

The cheesecloth was dumped into a special metal colander -- one with very small holes. After salt was added to the curds, they were set to drain. The colander was placed in a large bowl, and both were put into the refrigerator to cool and drain. Once the cottage cheese was as dry as you liked, it was put in the refrigerator with a clean cloth on top.

They did not want me to be anywhere close to the cottage cheese process. I was always in a hurry and far too messy and sometimes real dirty. So I was made to stand back and just watch. Of course, I was just right for working the slop bucket.

If the cottage cheese was dry, we added in a little cream. But that was about it. Once in a while Grandmother would put the cottage cheese in a tightly woven white cloth and squeeze out even more water. She called this Farmer's Cheese. Sometimes you just need something a little different on the table.

How did we eat cottage cheese, you ask? Often fresh green peppers, right out of the garden, were stuffed with cottage cheese. Warm tomatoes right out of the garden were stuffed with cold cottage cheese, too. About everybody had a cup of cottage cheese with every meal. All you had to do was cover the top with lots of black pepper, and the meal was ready for eating.

One of my favorite ways to eat cottage cheese is with hot brown beans with chopped green onions on the top, covered with a spoonful or two of chow-chow. All of this is served with a big slice of hot corn bread with lots of yellow cow butter. Now put a about a cup of good cold cottage cheese on the side of the plate all covered with black pepper.

The key here is to just to let the juices of the beans, butter and cottage cheese intermingle. There is nothing better. Most of time cottage cheese was a spring and early summer dish. The cows were on top of their milk then. We ate beans and cottage cheese instead of meat.

Mamaw's Cabbage Casserole

I think this cabbage recipe is another one that goes back to the idea that if you had it you ate it. Everything came from the garden or farm, or if the season was wrong from the country store. In this case, for example, Mamaw used yellow cheese from the country store.

Today we have a whole shelf of better cooking cheeses, so you can be creative. I usually use parmesan.

Here is what you need:

- One small head of cabbage. Take the core out and coarsely chop.
- Five tablespoons of yellow cow butter
- 1/4 cup of all purpose flour
- Two cups of whole milk
- Two eggs
- 1/2 cup of grated cheese
- One tablespoon of lemon juice
- One teaspoon salt

Now here is what you do:

- Preheat your oven to about 350 degrees.
- Boil the cabbage until it is limp and tender. Take the cabbage from the heat and pour it into a colander to drain.
- Melt the butter in a little saucepan and stir in the flour. Let the flour/butter come to a boil. Now stir in the milk.
- Pour the cabbage into a big bowl; add the butter, flour, lemon juice, eggs and salt. Stir until everything is evenly incorporated.
- Pour the cabbage into a Dutch Oven.
- Cover with black pepper if you like.
- Let the cabbage casserole bake for about 30 minutes or until it bubbles

Serving suggestions:

We always ate the cabbage casserole with corn bread, yellow cow butter, brown beans, sweet tea and fresh tomato slices.

Today, I like Grandmother's Cabbage Casserole with a glass of Sauvignon Blanc and grilled pork loin.

TREATS AND TREATMENTS

Lard and Lye Soap

The first week of December we made lard for cooking and lye soap. Lard was important stuff to us. Everyone on the hill and the whole community cooked with lard. Sometimes people would stop by and tell me there was a bucket of fat meat in the back of their truck, and say, "Carry it down to Shorty's; tell him that I will stop by on Saturday." Lots of people went together to make lard and soap.

To the close observer of life on River Ridge, there were many ways to tell the change of the season. For example, in late summer, when it got hot and the days were long the lard got strong or rancid, so you shifted to Crisco. You could tell when this happened, just like the shifting of the Earth on its axis. The biscuits were still good, but they were not the same. They did not have that same shine on top. The cakes made with real hog lard were even better than them Crisco ones.

Making lard was easy. Once the hog killing was past, and all the meat was cold enough to work, we set to trimming all the fat off. What was not put into the sausage was put into a big pile in the floor on a clean piece of plastic or piled up on a big table. Lard and soap cannot be made in the copper pot. Don't ask me why; it just ain't done that way. Yes sir, that is against all rules! Lard is made in the big, black, cast-iron pot -- the one used for boiling hams outside.

I started by cutting all of the leaf fat. (Big pieces of fat, just below the ribs, were called leaf lard.) I was to be careful and cut the leaf lard up into little squares like a checkerboard, then run them through the hand-cranked sausage grinder. I got this job because I was young and needed the exercise. These pieces needed to be real small, since they would be rendered down and made into cracklin for cornbread.

You don't want the fat meat with the skin on it to go in your cornbread; heavens no, you might break out a tooth or two. You eat the cracklin with the skin with lots of salt while drinking beer.

After I had about three or four buckets of leaf lard, pieces of fat from the middling, and anything trimmed off of the hams or shoulders, I started a small fire under the cast-iron pot. No water was added at all. I just put a few handfuls of ground-up fat into the pot and stirred it around with a wooden paddle. After a while it would start to cook and grease or liquid lard would appear. I'd add more raw fat and make the fire a little hotter. Soon, I had a pot full of rapidly boiling fat pieces and lard. I had to keep the liquid moving so that it did not burn, and also be real careful not to let the boiling lard splash out. If it hit you it could burn you all the way to the bone. What's more, if the liquid landed in the fire it would blaze up and possibly burn your leg all the way off.

Eventually, the grownups would look at it and tell me to pull the fire away—it was now lard. Standing there stirring the lard on a Saturday night, I thought I was ten feet tall. When I got a break I'd sneak over and get me one of those good, air-cooled Blue Ribbon Beers with a ring of frost on it. Once in a while somebody would tell me to step around behind the smokehouse so my mom wouldn't see me. "If she catches you, she will render all of us right there in that pot with the lard," they'd say.

We poured the hot lard through a strainer consisting of a wire screen like in a screen door and a second layer made of cheesecloth. The stuff that got caught on the screens was the cracklin, which were dumped into a big kittle and sorted, then covered with salt. As I said earlier, cracklin is a special ingredient for cornbread. Well, some of them -- those that weren't eaten hot with frosty cold beer.

About the time you got the lard strained and the cracklin salted, men came out of the woodwork carrying beer. We all set out by Grandmother's smokehouse on big wooden blocks to drink beer and eat fresh-cooked sausage and piles of newly salted cracklin. The beer did not need to be put in a refrigerator; the frost quietly settled around it and on everything, even us. These men could eat up a whole hog of sausage, so Mom and Grandmother made sure that most of the stuff was inside the house before the men got down to drinking and eating. You had to be careful not to break your teeth. Cold cracklin is very hard.

Sometimes when we made lard we also cooked sausage at the same time. The sausage was stuffed into small cloth bags Mom had made long before hog killing time. After they cooked in the lard pot they were hung up in the smokehouse with the other pork. This sausage was always eaten first. Now, that is good sausage.

We also made soap. I have tried my best to remember how we did it, and it is not coming to me. I do remember that all fall we saved up buckets of real white wood ashes to be mixed in with the boiling hog fat. Uncle Shorty had a big piece of pipe he filled with wood ashes. Very slowly he poured water into the pipe and let the ash and water mixture set for a week or longer. When we started making the soap, this chalky liquid was drained into the cooking fat before the pot started to boil. Uncle Shorty said that he was making homemade lye out of the wood ash.

They used store-bought Red Devil Lye, too, sometimes adding perfume to the boiling soap. I have even seen it with rose petals. I used lye soap to remove dandruff and treat poison ivy, and even tried it on skunk spray once, but it did not work. I remember the soap being very mild, and it did not dry out your skin like store-bought soap.

Hot Homemade Tea for the Upset Stomach

I remember going to the doctor once to have a hernia repaired. Other than for surgery, you were taken to Grandmother. Mamaw was old and experienced. She had raised ten of her own children and two more that she kind of took in along the way. She had seen all illnesses and successfully treated every one. She would pour stuff into you, dig things out of you and tie nasty things onto you all in the interest of good health. She was not as bad as Granny on the Beverly Hillbillies, but she ran a real close second.

If your stomach was upset she would brew up an herbal tea. Mom said the name of the plant was "Heal All." The tea was hot, green and nasty. It truly had little taste, but it was very slick and slimy in my mouth. You drank the stuff and in less than a week your stomach settled down. If you did not take the treatment, it took a full week for you to get better. If you had the real bad diarrhea, she would make the same herbal tea. But this time it was thick and black- looking with big hunks of the slimy weeds in it. You drank it hot to wash down as much

209

coconut as you could eat. I do not know if the increased fluids from that black nasty tea, the coconut or the pure fear that you was going to get another treatment made you better, but I got over the diarrhea and hoped it would not come back. The "Heal All" cure would make you stop running to the toilet.

I know from personal experience that Heal All was strong-tasting stuff and showed no mercy on the human body. I think that United States Army could make up a lot of it, put it in an airplane and spray our enemies. The war would be over in a few days. All enemies would be so locked up all the fight would just go out of them.

The Sore Throat

If Momma Ruth thought that you were going to get sick you were sent to Grandmother. She and Momma would get you under a light and pry open your mouth and look down your throat. If they could not see any inflammation, me, the sick one, was sent to the cellar for one salt brine pickle. They would not go, because the sauerkraut barrels and salt brine pickle crocks would make them sick. You see, I was already sick so it did not matter much. I was to bring the pickle back to Grandmother and Momma. They did not wash it off any. Nope, they just cut me a big 1/4 slice and instructed me to eat it.

If you jumped around a lot because the pickle was sour, nasty, slimy and salty, it was deemed you were okay. But if you did all the aforementioned things plus started to scream for milk, or for a hunk of cow butter or water and you started to cry, well maybe you did have a sore throat after all.

Treatment soon began. It was thought that lots of canned greens, lots of applesauce or anything that they could think up to make you need to go to the toilet seven or eight times right quick was good for you. Often Black Drought, if King's Cure plants were out of season; just anything to insure you got your bowels clean. "A good clean stomach meant the cold germs had nothing to hold onto down in your gut, and a good laxative removed all the hand holts for germs," said Elmer.

Another part of the treatment was a mouth and throat gargle. Grandmother would take a short walk down the path toward the pond or out toward Nelson's. In less than 20 minutes she would be back in the house boiling up a treatment. She had collected a large double handful off the "Heal All" plant. Yes, the same diarrhea treatment plant. After the tea had cooled down to room temperature you were made to gargle it a few times. It worked in less than an hour -- your sore throat was gone.

Childhood Diseases

When we were kids we truly did not go anywhere. Daddy said that he had traveled the seven seas and had seen the whole world during World War II, and there was not much else to see. We visited very few people other than those who lived right on River Ridge, or a family where a jar of moonshine just might be found. Then we were all best of friends or long-lost family members.

But there were times when we did go visiting. If another child in the area caught the whooping cough, measles, chicken pox or mumps, we either invited the family over or we went to their house for a visit.

Mom and Daddy wanted everyone to catch the chicken pox, mumps, three-day measles or the real measles all at one time and get it over with. Well, these measles parties worked. It was not uncommon for four or five of us kids to be sick at one time. The illness would go on for a few weeks. It seemed like Mom never slept or ate or even changed clothes. She was always there. She was just like that.

The Croup

When I was a young child, I caught an awful cold. Daddy said that I had the croup and my nonstop "barking" was preventing him from sleeping. Notice here, my cold and coughing was not so much hurting me as it was annoying him. Oh, now, Elmer was a compassionate person as long as you were not a bother to him. Well, I had to get over this cold fast before I went to really bothering Elmer. The hot bacon greasy treatment was a constant threat.

One of my younger siblings was evicted from his or her baby bed. The mattress was taken out and set up against the wall. Nothing was left but the bed springs. A hot plate with boiling water was set under the baby bed. You got it; I was put in the baby bed and told to set down on the springs. A heavy quilt was put over the top, and then a small jar of Vicks VapoRub was scraped into the hot water. When the water started to boil, I started to scream. It was hot and the steam was killing me.

Elmer said, "Stay in there; that snot has got to come out of you. I want air to go back into your head in places where air ain't gone in months."

214

Well, if the truth be known here, snot did come pouring out of me. My biggest worry was my eyes. My eyes were burning as much as my nose was running. He was right, but his way of articulating the situation could have been improved.

Pappy did not have a very good bedside manner. Life is funny; today I often use the expression "that snot has got to come out of there." I guess Elmer's teachings stuck with me.

Mom, Daddy, and Grandmother all took turns looking at me. They finally said that I had had enough, there was no more snot in me, and they let me out of the steam bath.

I was cured of the croup for a few days. But, others in the family started to cough, or "bark" as Elmer said. "Oh, I got to have some relief," he claimed.

Old Doctor Magnus from Blacksburg was called. Much later in life, Daddy described him as part human, doctor, part veterinary and all rough. Well Doctor Magnus made a house call to River Ridge. Believe it or not the baby bed and hot plate and steam were brought out. This time no Vicks VapoRub was used. All of us kids were put into the baby bed at one time. When the steam got to going real good and the kids started screaming to be let out, Old Doctor Magnus put a little jar of stuff in the water that made the Vicks taste like a T-Bone Steak. This stuff was bad. The snot began to roll.

"Keep them in there a little longer, you want to get all the snot out you can on the first treatment," instructed Doctor Magnus.

After a while we were all let out of the steam bed, and each of us was given a spoonful of medicine and put to bed. We slept for a long time without moving. When I woke up, I was truly over the croup.

Codeine is a wonderful medicine for the cough. Elmer was able to go back to sleeping too. I have often wondered if Dr. Magnus gave Elmer a double shot of the codeine to calm him down. He needed some sleep more than I did.

Grandmother stayed with us the whole time the Doctor was in the house. She might have been protecting us from the evils of modern medicine or just maybe she was trying to pick up a few new treatments. You just never knew about my Mamaw.

Doctors don't make house calls much anymore. I guess that is good. Once in a while, though, it might be good if they'd come to the sick. If they did, it might still hurt some. But, the pain and suffering would be less than what Mom and my Mamaw could inflict. Or even Uncle Shorty, who wanted you to run your head into the pump house until "all that stuff comes out." He just couldn't take "any more of that 'sniff-sniff' sound."

I am not going to use any real names here, but this story is truly as it was told to me. I have always hoped it was meant just to make me set still and do as the doctor or Grandmother told me. Well, here goes.

There was a fine gentleman in my community that had a very coarse speech pattern. Shorty, Elmer and others said

216

that when this man was a very young child he had the croup, too. He just could not stop coughing. It got so bad that he was keeping everyone awake for weeks. So one morning while he was asleep and coughing with his mouth open, his father poured hot sausage grease down his throat so he would stop coughing.

I do hope that every word is false, truly I do. But I set in the baby bed on bare springs and heard Elmer tell Mother and Mamaw that the next treatment may have to be the "Sausage Grease" treatment. Why, I would breathe very deeply. Shorty said that you might not talk well after the Sausage Grease treatment, but you'd surely sleep well and the snot can get out too. I think that we either got better or grew up or we would have died! The lovely Miss Gail often says I was raised by wolves.

Bad Cuts, Sores and Rough Scrapes

A country boy getting cut isn't anything new or something to even be talked about. Everybody walked around with some form of almost life-threatening wound. Now, there were two standard treatments for about everything. First off there was the store-bought medicine -- things like Merthiolate or Raleigh Salve.

Merthiolate could be purchased at any store. There was always a large display of the stuff. On the medicine shelf there would be a small row of bandages, nine or ten kinds of laxatives -- things like Milk of Magnesia, Ex-lax, Black Draft and the like -- and right beside the laxatives there would be three or four types of wound treatments -- things like turpentine, Mercurochrome and Merthiolate. If you stood back from the medicine shelf and just thought for a minute, you'd figure out about the only illnesses a boy on River Ridge ever got were constipation and cuts.

Another not store-bought treatment was Raleigh Salve. A

man that lived near McCoy came around with an old van just filled with all kinds of wonderments. In the fall he would have boxes of sweet potatoes, and there were a few cast-iron frying pans. Once in while, he'd have watermelons and cantaloupes. He even had small jars of liver cures for men. (I think that the liver cure was just pint bottles of store-bought bourbon he was reselling.) The Raleigh Salve man also carried an assortment of hairbrushes and ribbons for the ladies. He sold things out of his truck to everyone up and down the road. There was something to address everybody's needs! He even had new and old dirty magazines for sale.

When he stopped, you just never knew what he had for sale. He never had the same stock except for Raleigh Salve, which would cure anything. I mean everything. We rubbed Raleigh salve into barbed wire cuts on hogs. We rubbed Raleigh Salve on chapped milk cow teats. We rubbed it on people's heads to chase out the head lice. Once Old Fanny, our beautiful old plow horse, was rubbed raw on her back from the plow harness. Uncle Shorty went looking for Mr. McCall, we called him the Raleigh Salve Man. We washed Old Fanny's back with warm water and lye soap and dried her off with a burlap sack and rubbed on six or seven handfuls of Raleigh Salve and turned her loose. "In less than three weeks she was solid as Herbert Hoover's Dollar," Uncle Shorty said.

With healing powers exhibited like this, Raleigh Salve was rubbed on everything from scratches, to bruises, to small and large cuts to sore muscles. Momma said that it just might have saved me from polio once or twice.

219

Bee Stings

We truly did not like to get stung by a bee. I did not mind too much that the bee was most likely going to die, and for a fat little boy the pain wasn't much either. I did not even mind having a bad itching knot on my body for a day or two. I just hated to tell Momma. She always got one of the saddest looks on her face -- not for me, but for what she was about to do.

"Well you kids are more important to me than I am to myself," she would say.

I knew what was about to happen. She would break off a big chew of plug chewing tobacco and set to chewing it. The more she chewed the greener she started to look. Just a few seconds before she started to get sick on her stomach, she spat out that big mouthful of chewing tobacco and flopped it down on my bee sting. Then she stepped around the corner of the house and started throwing up.

She just never did get the hang of chewing tobacco. I truly felt sorrier for her than me. I was over the bee sting in an hour. Mom was not over my bee sting and the tobacco until the next day.

Sore Legs

When I was about six or seven years old, my legs hurt and throbbed all the time. Grandmother said that I had growing pains. Castor oil and cod liver oil was her recommended treatment. Tootie said I was growing too fast and should eat more honey, greens and potatoes. Miss Ester said that it was the meanness working its way out, and I ort to have my butt busted more often. Aunt Letty said that I needed to set in hot water more, so I got a bath every week or as often as Mom could catch me. After being drenched with castor oil and cod liver oil, greens, hot water and ass-busting, my legs still hurt.

Poor old Mom sat for long periods of time and rub my legs. It seemed like it was for hours. She would take a big handful of "Raleigh Salve" in her hands and rub them until it was all gone.

"If it has helped some of those cuts you have had, I just know it will cure your legs. I think that I can keep this from turning into polio, or something worse," Mom said. "I have had a damn hard time getting you this big; I ain't going to give up on you now."

After all these treatments, I started to get a little better. All of the old ladies were convinced their treatment worked, and I lived only because of their advice.

As for me and Momma, I think it was her constant rubbing of my legs with that smelly Raleigh Salve and her determination that I was not going to catch polio that did the trick.

After I was pretty much on the mend, Mom jokingly told me, "I was afraid to let your grandmother get real close to you. She might decide that one or both of your legs would need to come off. She might have cut them off, too. You just never know about your grandmother."

I think that I had a case of Osker-Slaughters, but no one had even heard of that back in 1955.

A Boil and Bad Bumps

One of the things I have noticed as I have gotten older is almost no one ever gets boils or great big inflamed bumps today. As a child I had very few boils, but did catch real big bumps from insect bites and very deeply embedded thorns and briars. Grandmother said big bumps was a sign that you were too mean and you did not take enough baths. If you ended up with a boil that would not come to a head, Grandmother tied a large piece of salt-cured fat meat over it. You wore the fat-meat bandage for two, sometimes three days. After the skin got a puckered look about it, Mom held me down or set on me while Grandmother doctored on me. Which translates into, she set about taking a big sewing needle to dig out whatever was down in there. Once, I think they dug out good skin from the other side of my leg.

Under the fat meat, after a day or two, my skin was white, wrinkly and right irritated. All of this irritation made the boil come to a head. Here is the part that I truly did not like. Mom would set on me again, and sometimes Aunt Letty or Tootie were called in to help hold me down. Grandmother took one of her sewing needles and stuck it in the firebox of the cook stove

223

for a second or two and started to dig out the infected center of the boil.

"Now you just might as well hold still; that infected core has got to come out."

They had no mercy on a little fat boy, even if he was big for his age. I began to think that treatment was far worse than the illness.

When I was about 30 years old I had a boil on my left forearm. The doctor did surgery in his office. He used a sterile scalpel and lots of clean gauze. He even gave me antibiotics. The experience was nothing like being held down by old women and having them just take to digging in my skin. Today, I think I would die of shock. Back then about all I could think about was trying to run fast and far. But they were just too heavy. My poor old mom would cry, but she would not turn loose of me.

The Earache and a Voodoo Man

When I was a little boy I had the earache all of the time. Even today, doctors inform me that part of my hearing loss is due to lots of ear infections as a child. I walked around about all the time with a big hunk of cotton in my ears. About every time I passed Grandmother she would fill my ears with sweet oil. She was a great believer in sweet oil. Mom, on the other hand, filled my ears with alcohol to wash out the oil and to watch me jump and squirm. It burned and I did both, jump and squirm, that is.

Mamaw had lots of faith in clean ears. It did not matter if you had just washed them; they were not clean until she said they were clean. She was old and arthritic, but she could run you down to check your ears. She would take a washcloth and wrap it around a ten-penny nail head to scrub out your ears. She got stuff out, too, -- things like earwax, red meat and eardrum tissue. "Now they are clean," she would say.

Well one day -- I am thinking I was maybe six or seven

225

years old -- we had gone to the community of Wake Forest. Not the community with a University in it, but the one where a lot of black people lived. Well, we had not gone to Wake Forest to visit or to check on the weather. In fact, asking questions and talking slowed us down on our mission to buy bootleg licker. I always thought that it was funny that when they bought moonshine from a black person it was called "Old Alligator Bait." When you bought white lightning from white folks, it was just called "Shine."

Uncle Lake, he was the more worldly of the brothers, said that back before World War II, once in awhile you could find a bottle of licker named "Old Alligator Bait." The label on the bottle had two black men setting there by the river with an alligator just a-smiling. Alligator Bait was powerful stuff and just made you smile.

After the bootleg was bought there would be all the time in the world to talk. Daddy, Shorty, Nelson, Mod and Gilbert had made their purchase, and the pace of our mission slowed down a bit. I looked the moonshine jar over and there was no mention made of any alligators. I figured one day when I was older I would understand this better.

There is a wide space in the road near the base of the big hill right beside the creek. We were parked in the gathering place when one of the men came over to me and asked, "How long have you had that earache? Every time I see you, you got that cotton stuck in your ear."

226

Mr. Bookings was the local healer; he and my grandmother were in the healing profession. He was part healer with a little turn toward voodoo. Here's what happened:

He sets me up on the hood of his car and pulls the cotton from my ear and looks down deep into the small, dark ear hole. He takes out a can of cigarette papers and a tin of Prince Albert. He rolls up a nice fat cigarette. Once he gets the cigarette fired up hot, he draws up a big deep breath and blows the smoke down into my ear. He does this until the cigarette is smoked up. Then he sticks the cotton back in my ear.

"You don't want all that goodness to get out of there. That will cure that sore ear. I have wanted to get a-holt of your head for long time. Now you will be all right."

To be honest it did feel better for a little while, or possibly I just wanted it to be better. After awhile it was right back to hurting. One day my ears just stopped hurting on their own. Maybe cigarette smoke just takes a few years to work. I have heard of slow healing.

I had always heard of Mr. Bookings, too. He was the medical man and also the local wart-witcher. After the ear treatment, I thought that it would be good to have a few warts. Not big ones just small ones, the kind that could be charmed off real easy.

Unfortunately, I never did get the warts. But, I did see Mr. Bookings set to talking to other people's warts while he rubbed them real easy. Somehow, some way, those warts did go away.

As I got older I started to think that possibly he was more of a voodoo medical man or something. I asked Shorty and Daddy, and they just said it was a gift he had got. I still never got warts. Maybe watching him was kind of like taking a polio shot or something.

Now if you were worried about warts and went to Grandmother with warts, she had a preventive treatment. Aunt Tibb and Aunt Edith both told me that wart removal or prevention wasn't that hard. Mamaw had you wash a lot of dishes, rub your hands with lots of fat meat, wipe off the fat meat with an old, holey dishtowel (a new one would not work), and bury the dishtowel under a big rock. Mamaw's treatment worked, too. Also, every once in awhile you repeated this treatment against warts. The more often, the better. Aunt Edith laughed and said it worked, because she never did get the warts.

A Local Boy and the Chocolate Bar

I like to call this young man "Local Boy," because he is. Besides that, if I put his name down someone just might not like to hear about their grandpaw, or me, for that matter.

I was in the second grade and one of my classmates ate my candy bar. Someone took the candy bar right out of my desk and ate it and left me nothing but the candy wrapper. A few days later it happened again.

One afternoon when me and Uncle Nelson were feeding his hogs and smoking up some homemade cigarettes, I told him about my candy bar situation. When we got back to his and Aunt Toots' house, Nelson went into the back room and brought out a very small bottle of liquid.

"Now take this stuff with you to school and just put a few drops on a candy bar and leave the candy setting," he said. "In just a few minutes you will know exactly who your candy bar thief is. He'll get sick and start to shitting. Why, he will even shit out his teeth unless he is holding to them real tight."

About this time, Aunt Tootie came into the room and wanted to know what we were doing playing with that bottle of croton oil.

"Nelson, you know better than to play with that stuff. You could kill Harmie with that." (I was Harmie back then.)

Toot made me wash my hands, and she put the little bottle back on the shelf. Now, I did not know what croton oil was (still is) or where one got it, and it did sound right drastic for my situation. But it did give me an idea.

The next morning at school I set a full box of 12 squares of Ex-Lax on the radiator to warm up. Once they were soft, I took out a Hershey's Chocolate Bar, the one with the little square pieces. With a Popsicle stick, I rubbed the Ex-Lax across the top of the candy bar. I guess I used at least eight or ten pieces of Ex-Lax. I carefully slid the candy bar back into the wrapper and set it in plain view. In just a few minutes all the other school busses started to arrive. In just few more minutes my Hershey bar was gone, and I still did not see who got it.

Well, school went on and got started, but I could not do anything for wondering if my plan for finding the candy thief would work. In less than an hour, the "Local Boy," who will remain nameless, needed to go to the bathroom and I mean right now. He came back to the room looking pale. Then he had to go again. In just a few minutes the principal was in our room. She had called his mother to come and get him and take him home between trips to the bathroom.

His mom came and got him and when he left the room he looked right straight at me. I said nothing, not one word. I was scared, because if my mother learned what I had done, I knew she would do the same to me.

Well, all of the mothers on the hill were called in for an expanded diagnosis. It was pretty much agreed that there was something in his stomach acting up, and it needed to be brought out of there. Someone went for King's Cure weeds. When "Young Man" came back to school, he was thinner and paler. But you could leave an unwrapped candy bar on any desk, right out in plain view, and it was safe. "Young Man" wasn't going to touch it, much less eat it.

Later, his mother told my mother that he had caught one of the worse diarrheas that ever was had. "I thought at the time he was going to pass his teeth. Everything you made him eat just came out the other end."

This wasn't a home treatment, but it worked. I told Uncle Nelson what I had done, "Whoa! Damn you boy, you could have killed him. Mixing Ex-Lax and King's Cure might just make a man want to fill the toilet with one setting. Don't do that anymore."

Sicknesses That Always Seemed to be Bothering Dad

Dad was always worrying about his stomach and lower parts. He was known to drink a large swallow of mineral oil every day of his life. When he ran out of mineral oil he would down a bottle of Milk of Magnesia. He said that it healed him from within. It was known to cure his "Scavilo." (There is no known spelling of this word, and no explanation, either.)

Elmer said this was not the easiest digestive disease to treat, because it caused the formation of a thick, yellow ring around one's butt. Once you were cured of the Scavilo, you were prone to catch the Opto-recto-mitus. (Again there is no known spelling for this word that I am aware of.) Elmer said this is a condition where the optic nerve is firmly attached to the rectum. It gave one a very negative outlook on things. The treatment was a regular drenching of oneself with mineral oil.

Again this is my father speaking, not me. Also, one needed to always be on the lookout for symptoms of Assfaceia. This, too, is a digestive disorder that occurs when one's face is so similar

232

in appearance to one's butt that the content of one's stomach does not know which way to go and can cause blindness.

Pidovia was another one of Elmer's illnesses. This one did seem to give him a great number of problems, but a good sound dose of mineral oil could keep most of the illness at bay.

One time Daddy was in Radford Hospital. Something was wrong with him. Now that may sound kind of funny to you -- "something was wrong with him" -- but this was the way it was with Elmer. You see, he would go to the doctor if he was sick, but he would not tell the doctor where it hurt.

"I am the one sick here, and you are the doctor. If you are any count you will find it," Elmer would explain.

Pappy was in the Radford Hospital for something, and I do not know for what. Radford Hospital may not have known, either. But, the one thing they did know is that they had him on a strict water and toothpick diet. He kept gaining weight, so they kept cutting his food intake, and he still kept gaining weight. One day, they lost him from the hospital and had to go looking for him. One of the nurses saw him out of the hospital window. They found him across the road standing in someone's garden in his hospital gown; his butt was catching some sun and breeze. He was grazing on cucumbers, tomatoes and peppers. Those were his favorites.

Well, the nurses coaxed him out of the garden and back across the street and into the hospital bed.

"Mr. Lytton," the nurse said," don't you know you can't go slipping off without letting me know about it?"

Daddy said, "I did not know that you like cucumbers, tomatoes and peppers that much."

Well, he was not eating anything at all in the hospital. His weight was still going up. Then Daddy confessed that he had brought no clothes with him. Instead he had brought a suitcase full of peanut butter and cheese nabs, "just in case you tried to starve me down."

Did he get well? Hell, I do not know if he was even sick. But he did not get hungry. We later learned that, today, Elmer would be treated for Irritable Bowel Syndrome.

A Spring Tonic for Everyone

Now, I just told you that Daddy was bothered by many ailments of the stomach. Being a good father, he did not want to pass on any stomach ailments to his children. Each and every spring you got a spring tonic "guaranteed to clean you out and get rid of anything up in there," Elmer would say. Yes sir, Daddy was lacking in some areas, but he lacked nothing in colorfulness.

The overall goal was to have you running to the toilet half-bent over, holding your stomach and screaming, "get the hell out of the way." Every March or April, Elmer thought that we needed this "Spring Tonic." Now, don't get me wrong, parts of this little ritual were truly fun. But, knowing what this was all building up to kept me mindful of the consequences. I truly did know what, "I am going to clean you out and start you out all over again," meant, and it was not fun.

All willing and unwilling participants were loaded into the back of one or two pickup trucks and hauled to a place along the railroad, a place that Daddy and Shorty called Pepper Station. Sometime in the past a railroad train station was located on this spot. Daddy handed each of us a cloth bag or a small sack,

235

and then made sure that all of us had our pocketknives.

Next he gave a good, sound botany lesson on edible plants and what poison ivy looked like. We spent more time on poison ivy than edible plants. We were to focus our attention on plants like wild mustard, flat field cresses, creasy greens, young lamb's quarter, dandelions, chicory and two or three types of wild lettuce. Hell, you could have put a thistle in the sack and no one would have known or cared so long as they did not get stuck by it. Why did it matter? All you were going to do was eat it.

One of the fun things for me was the running stories that Daddy and Shorty kept telling back and forth as we went. It was like a little piece of history. The one story that always amazed me was about an old man that worked for the Virginian Railroad. Each morning he would start out walking from the Whitethorn Station to the Pepper Station and back. From Whitethorn to Pepper is nine miles one way. His job was to do minor maintenance along the track. He did things like replace missing spikes; tighten loose rail bolts, chunk gravels back under the rails in places where they were getting pushed out. Now you might be thinking that anyone could do this. Well, yes, I could tighten the bolts and chunk the gravel. The tough part was he had to carry everything with him -- a spike hammer, a shovel, a few spikes, a spud wrench, a ballast fork and anything else he might have needed. Shorty said he had it all in a heavy sack slung over his shoulder. Keep in mind this was an 18-mile walk every day.

Sometimes I think that they were just shooting me a line of bull just to keep me from complaining about carrying my wild lettuce sack. All the while we were walking down the railroad picking greens and dodging trains. Every once in awhile we stopped for a little rest. That was when Daddy would check your bags of greens. He was not checking what you picked; he was just checking how much you had picked. He would take his fist and pack them down. Your full bag now had only an inch of greens in the bottom. Every once in awhile a train would come by. It was a welcome sight. We set our bags on the ground and settled back to count the number of railroad cars and just enjoy the wind generated by the train.

Another little game that Daddy and Shorty liked for me to play was to see if I could touch my nose to a coal car as it passed. You had to wait until the train was in a real hard pull; it would be going real slow pulling up the mountain. Then, all I had to do was inch myself as close to a passing car as I dared, then stretch out my neck and stick out my nose ever so slowly and touch the car. Then I had to draw my nose back real quick, before it got broke off or scrubbed off. If you had a spot of dirt or railroad grease on the end of your nose you did well; no dirty nose you lost. I never saw them even try. But they would start laughing as soon as I started getting close to the train.

As I got older, it dawned on me that there are three or four large exterior braces on a coal car. If I had hit one of those I most likely would have had my nose broke or I might possibly have been killed. But, men of River Ridge just did not think about things like that; they just saw the humor in seeing me stretch out my neck to touch the car with my nose.

Well, we picked greens from Pepper to the White Rock. There we walked through the railroad gate and into Shorty's field. Yes, we were still picking greens. As for me, the closer I got to the house the more I botanized. Well, that is what I called it. I just picked any wild green plant that looked like one could eat it. They were going to get boiled anyway, and to me a weed is a weed. So I just keep up the botanizing. After a few mash downs or pickings, everything kind of looked like it had already been eaten anyway.

When we got home, we set about washing them greens. They were not called greens; they were "them greens." After we worked hard to pick them, I guess they took on a life of their own. I knew that they were going to come alive in me soon. I did not care. I had had a lot of fun, and I had had a spring tonic before.

Mom and Daddy would set two or three dishpans of water on a table in the backyard. Each leaf had to be looked over for bugs and dirt. Then each leaf had to be passed through the three pans of water. In just a few minutes Mom and Dad would leave the cleaning to me. They went in the house to start the boiling and cooking. I was a faster washer than either of them. You see, I would put whole handfuls of greens in the tub at a time. Worms, bugs and greens went into the pile. They were all going to be cooked anyway.

Mom would set a three-gallon kettle to boiling. In the kettle she put about a gallon of water and one pound or more of salted fat meat. The fat meat was needed for flavor. Mom added in some extra salt if needed. She then came out to a pick up a pile of "them greens" about the size of a wheelbarrow. Slowly, she put them in the big kettle. In just a minute, they cooked down and she added in some more. Once you got so many greens in the kettle that not one more would fit, they were left to boil for while. You could always tell when they were done. They took on a kind of slick look. You could not tell one green from another. Yes, they were boiled into a slick, non-recognizable pan of something kind of like compost.

Just before the greens had finished cooking, I was sent to the garden. I was to pick a few small green onions. They had not been planted long. All of them were small. Another of life's decisions: was I to wash them in the same pan that we used to wash the greens? About the same method of washing was used. While I was onion picking, Daddy was making cornbread, one of my favorites. Soon it would be time eat. I knew what was coming soon.

I was given a big dish of "them greens," sometimes called "the tonic." Others just called it "the treatment." If you were lucky you got a small piece of the salt pork fat, too. You put a small handful of fresh onions on the top. You covered your greens with black pepper, more salt and lots of vinegar. While that was working together, you cut a large chunk of fresh yellow cow butter and got it between the two halves of your cornbread before it cooled off any. You wanted the yellow butter to be able to soak into the bread. Top this off with a glass or two of fresh, cold sweet milk. If the butter had just been made, you could have cold buttermilk instead of sweet milk. But, you had to race Daddy to get it. He was large, but he was real fast when it came to buttermilk. If you were lucky enough to get the buttermilk, you would cover the top of the glass with black pepper and a few slices of green onion tops.

To be honest, it was a fine meal. I could eat two or three dishes of "them greens." The walk in the cool, clean air always made me hungry. After a while, they took to working on you. Daddy loved to see you running as fast as you could for the toilet, hollering: "Get out of the way and fast."

He seemed to know stomach sounds, too. He did not want to hear any normal stomach sound. He wanted sounds of severe distress. If he even thought that you could differentiate between urination and defecation, you needed another dish. (They did not use those terms; they were a little more to the point, if you know what I mean.) In a sick kind of way, when you were running for your life, Daddy would sit under the oak tree and laugh. Sometimes Shorty joined him. I think that they sat there so they would not have as far to run.

Years later, I am employed by The University of Tennessee at Martin as a research agronomist. The year is 1982. That spring we plant no less than 200 clover plots. In July everything is in full bloom and the fields are out of this world with flowers. "Why they look good enough to eat," said a young man named Frank

Lee McElroy. Everyone just looks at one another. I suggest someone needs to make a trip to the store a pick up bottle of blue cheese salad dressing; the rest of us will pick clover. We can meet up at the greenhouse in an hour, and we will make up a clover salad. We picked red clover, crimson clover, arrowleaf clover and a half dozen more varieties. We even throw in a dozen or more varieties of alfalfa.

Well, we wash the stuff and mix in a few tomatoes and onion. We pour everything into a big tub and add the salad dressing. Everyone digs in. Now, to be right honest, it is not the best thing I ever ate. Some of these clover varieties have a green, sappy, maybe a wild-like taste, but down it all goes. After lunch we go back to mowing our clover plots. One by one each of us makes a run for the toilet. Most of us make it. Some have to make do with the tall corn plots. Some do not make it at all. No matter where you get caught you can hear the moaning and groaning.

As I set on the seat of ease, I had to laugh right out loud as my stomach cramped and twisted. I had been in this same situation before, and damn if I wasn't here again. Frankie said that we did not wash the clover enough, and we all caught food poisoning. I had to laugh again. We all caught the poisoning all right. We had caught the shits from eating too much cow feed. I have at least two or maybe three stomachs, and I would need at least four or maybe five to eat that real pretty clover.

The entire farm crew laughed for weeks. Being a true Appalachian American comes with responsibilities. One of the old men working on the farm crew said, "I reckon that you boys could shit through a needle's eye if you was a mind to." Them old men were as colorful as my daddy. It is a small world isn't it? Elmer would have said the exact same thing.

Today, I try not to take too much spring tonic. I just don't think I am tough enough anymore. One thing for sure. I do not have any "pidovia"!

PRACTICAL JOKES
AND
WONDERFUL PEOPLE

Jimmy Bland
Tried to Skeer Momma

As an adult I can look back on the relationship shared between Jimmy Bland and my mother and just chuckle. Today Mother Ruth is in a nursing home. Gail and I visit her, as do other friends and family. But, in some ways the visits from Jimmy Bland make Mom smile the happiest. He brings her a large bag of Cheetos, and they set and tell the old stories until both their fingers and lips are yellow. In Mom's eyes Jimmy Bland can do no wrong.

One morning, years ago, everyone was setting around in the kitchen watching as Mom cooked breakfast. Jimmy just stepped out the back door and lit a whole pack of firecrackers and set them under the kitchen window. When they went off Mom started hopping, cussing and pitching the corned beef hash around with the spoon. When the fireworks stopped outside; the fireworks started inside. Mom was madder than a wet hen, and she took to cussing. Jimmy just laughed at her, and in a few minutes she was back fixing his breakfast. If I had done this she would have disowned me, but not Jimmy.

245

Forty-five years later they still share the old stories, talk about Jimmy's family and eat them orange Cheetos.

I never cease to be amazed by the people you meet and the impact they have on our lives. Jimmy was good at hog killing, a good canoer and a great firecracker pitcher. But, in some ways Jimmy seemed to calm Mother's nerves. She needed that when we were kids and sure welcomes it now that all of us are more in contact with the real world.

Mom always fed Jimmy fried duck eggs and chicken-fried deer steaks for breakfast, and he never knew.

"You can feed your son them duck eggs and deer steaks, but you are not going to trick me into eating that," Jimmy would say.

Mom would cook Jimmy's eggs and steak first, then she would cook mine, so as not to contaminate his eggs and chicken fried steak. Mom never said a word and neither did I. We both ate and enjoyed our breakfast.

Duck eggs are a little larger than hen eggs. The yellow is a very bright orange. Momma always said they were just richer. On River Ridge everyone cooked with duck eggs. They made very yellow pancakes, and the regular cakes were yellow, too. Few families ate straight duck eggs, though. It seemed like everybody preferred chicken eggs.

I think we ate them because they were free. If you took your time, you could find ducks' nests near the old pond in the hollow. You could get an egg or two every day. If you needed a lot, you went over the hill to one of the local farms and Miss Connie would instruct you on where to look for her duck eggs. Today, as I reflect back, I think we were poorer than I realized, but it doesn't seem to have hurt me that much.

Here is what you need:

- Four or five venison round steaks
- A dish of flour
- Salt and pepper
- A meat pulverizer or hammer
- Lard
- A big cast-iron skillet.

Now, here is what you do:

- Put three or four tablespoons of lard in the big skillet to heat up.
- On the wooden board, hammer the deer steak until it is at least 1/4 larger in diameter than its original size. Remove the round bone, too.
- When the lard is hot, roll the deer steak in flour and put it in the hot lard. (Move it around a little.)
- Cook until the meat is brown on both sides.
- Serve right out of the pan.

The First Pecan Pie

I did not see this, but I do wish that I had. I only heard this one told over and over by my uncles, my dad, and their friends. I do think that it fits in here. So here goes.

Back in the late 1920s or early 1930s the Merita Bread Truck had started digging through the deep potholes and cavernous gullies in the dirt road toward McCoy. Locals had heard for months that they were trying to make the run to Long's Shop, a regular stop on the bread delivery route.

One day when all the locals came to the store to catch up on the news and gossip, there was two already sliced loaves of Merita Bread. Every person that came in picked up a loaf and touched it, smelled of it and carefully looked it over. Finally someone bought a loaf of bread, and soon thereafter the second one was sold. I cannot tell you who these groundbreaking bread buyers were, but thereafter eight or ten loaves of bread were sold each week.

Then one day there was a new bakery item left by the Merita bread man. The label said "pecan pie." Just like they did with the first loaves of bread, everyone that came in looked at it, picked it up and smelled it. Well, no one in their right state of mind was going spend three cents on an unknown thing like a store-bought pecan pie.

Some of my uncles and another local man pooled their money and came up with three cents and purchased it. They set the pie outside on a carbide can and dared the next man to come through the door to eat it. There were no takers for free pie.

Then there came Watcher Havens. He was known to be a little off and right down different, all the while keeping at least one eye on you, hence the nickname "Watcher." Well, Uncle Delmer said, "Hay, Watcher, wanna try to eat this here first store-bought pecan pie?"

Watcher picked up the pie. "You all buy me a cold Pepsi Cola to wash it down, and I'll eat her for you."

Well, everyone started to dig through their pockets and pool their money. They had almost enough money when Mr. Long, the storeowner, said he'd make up the difference cause he wanted to see Watcher eat the thing, too.

A good, cold Pepsi was set on the adjoining carbide can and the pecan pie was peeled out of the paper. Watcher took a good-size bite, chewed it hardily and washed it down with a long drink from the Pepsi.

In total silence, this was repeated over and over. Finally, the pie and Pepsi were all gone.

Uncle Delmer said, "Well?"

Watcher took his shirtsleeve and wiped off his mouth and said, "Well, I will just tell you the pie is might good. But the crust is a might tough. But might good, too."

The next week when the Merita Bread man came, about everybody that could come was waiting for him. As soon as one of the pecan pies was placed on the counter, Uncle Lake bought it. Right there in the store he unpeeled the paper wrapper, and it fell in the floor. The Merita man said, "You can go on and eat it. That there is a cardboard tray. You can't eat that anyways; why it might choke a fellow's gut or something."

"Cardboard tray?" everyone said. The Merita man picked up the pie and showed the group the cardboard pie tray.

Everyone had a good laugh. First off, no one knew what cardboard even was. They kept on laughing at Watcher. He had eaten the pecan pie and the cardboard tray, too. Yes, I reckon the crust was just a might tuff.

THE SWEETNESS
OF TIME

Some Things Just Live On Even Though They Never Were

I found it hard to get started on this last recipe and story, until I was helping my mother assemble a display of her life for the folks at the nursing home. I opened an old picture album, and a long lost, forgotten recipe fell to the floor. When I picked it up and read it, I realized that some things just live on even though they never were.

My grandmother had written this down many years ago and given it to my Mother. She had filed it away for an afternoon like the one we were experiencing. It was for something I have never eaten: "Honeysuckle Jelly."

I did like the fresh mint and spearmint jelly that both Mother and Mamaw made, and I'm pretty sure they used this same recipe.

Here is what you need:

- A large grocery bag full of honeysuckle flowers
- Two cups of boiling water
- 1/4 cup of lemon juice
- Four cups of sugar
- Three ounces of liquid pectin
- A one gallon cast-iron Dutch oven

Now, here is what you do:

- Be mindful of the heat. This jelly cooks quickly.
- Put all of the flowers in a pan of boiling water for no more than one minute
- Take out two cups of blanched honeysuckle flowers. Lightly push them down into the cup. Measure but do not mash them hard
- Get two cups of water boiling, but not a high boil
- Add all the flowers, the lemon juice and sugar
- Let the mixture just come back to a low boil. Keep an eye on the pan, for the sugar might stick. Boil for no more than two minutes or until the sugar has melted.
- Add in the pectin and let it boil for no more than three minutes
- Pour the hot jelly into jars.

It is funny how life just moves in a circle. I have a granddaughter. She is eight years old. You drop her off in a field or on a roadside, and she can smell out every honeysuckle vine. She can just stand by the vine picking honeysuckle flowers and eating the sweet nectar from the bottom of each blossom and give a big smile after each flower.

It made me just think back about my Mamaw. I never saw her eat honeysuckle flowers; I sure did eat them and sometimes still do. Mamma must have, too, or she would not have written down the recipe for Honeysuckle Jelly.

Some things just live on; kind of like you are just programmed to eat honeysuckle flowers.

Made in the USA
Charleston, SC
06 January 2011